AVIATION SOCIAL SCIENCE: RESEARCH METHODS IN PRACTICE

Aviation Social Science: Research Methods in Practice

MARK W. WIGGINS
University of Western Sydney, Macarthur
CATHERINE STEVENS
University of Western Sydney, Macarthur

Routledge
Taylor & Francis Group

LONDON AND NEW YORK

First published 1999 by Ashgate Publishing

Published 2016 by Routledge
2 Park Square, Milton Park, Abingdon, Oxfordshire OX14 4RN
711 Third Avenue, New York, NY 10017, USA

First issued in paperback 2016

Routledge is an imprint of the Taylor & Francis Group, an informa business

British Library Cataloguing in Publication Data
Wiggins, Mark W.
    Aviation social science: research methods in practice
    - (Studies in aviation psychology and human factors)
    1.Aeronautics - Human factors - Research
    I.Title II.Stevens, Catherine
    629.1'3'072

Library of Congress Cataloging-in-Publication Data
Wiggins, Mark W.
    Aviation social science: research methods in practice / Mark
W. Wiggins and Catherine Stevens.
        p.   cm. -- (Studies in aviation psychology and human factors)
        Includes bibliographical references and index.
        ISBN 1-84014-966-3 (hbk.)
        1. Aircraft industry--Research. 2. Social sciences--Research.
    I. Stevens, Catherine. II. Title. III. Series.
    HD9711.A2W54 1999
    300'.7'2--dc21   99-16516
                                                                                CIP

ISBN 13: 978-1-138-25048-2 (pbk)
ISBN 13: 978-1-84014-966-1 (hbk)

Contents

List of Tables, Figures and Boxes

Acknowledgements

In the preparation of this book, we sought the assistance of a number of researchers and practitioners within the aviation environment to comment on the various drafts. We are indebted to them for their time and effort, and the interest they took in reading the material. In particular, we would like to thank Irene Henley, Michelle Parbery, Lee Kirschner, Amanda Howard, Rob Lee, Deborah Egan, Monica Martinussen, Peter Renshaw, Richard Heath, Graham Beaumont, David Hunter, Paul Satchell, David O'Hare, and Adele Hills. We would also like to thank John Hindley for his assistance in the production of the book. The authors are pleased to acknowledge the assistance of the Department of Aviation Studies and the Faculty of Arts and Social Sciences at the University of Western Sydney, Macarthur in the preparation of the manuscript. Finally, we would like to thank our families and colleagues for their unflagging support and encouragement.

Foreword

This is an important book that will meet a long-standing need in the aviation community. The undertaking of applied human factors research in aviation is a difficult and challenging task, particularly in the context of regular public transport operations. Commercial and operational constraints, as well as the difficulty in obtaining access to simulators and experimental participants such as pilots, air traffic controllers and maintenance personnel, and the potentially high costs involved, are obstacles to meaningful research that addresses operational, human factors issues.

Traditionally, there has been a barrier between the operational aviation and academic environments that has inhibited the free exchange of information and ideas. Nonetheless, the two communities can no longer afford to function in isolation. The skills and expertise in both aviation and academia are required to address critical human factors issues in the aviation environment.

Although human factors remains the most significant area in aviation safety, many of the research skills needed to address human factors issues are not widely known or practiced in the operational environment. Conversely, the knowledge and experience of airline operations is generally not found in the academic environment. However, academics can provide invaluable assistance to aviation personnel who seek to conduct applied research. In the absence of such assistance, 'research' is often conducted without a theoretical basis, has used poorly controlled protocols, and can be methodologically and statistically flawed. To redress this situation, a combination of academic an operational strengths is required. Just as the application of the laws of aerodynamics is critical to the design and operation of aircraft, so the theoretical and practical strategies presented in this book are essential for successful research and the resolution of critical human factors issues in aviation.

This book has been written to bridge the gap that can exist between the academic and non-academic world in terms of operational research. The intention is to acquaint operational practitioners with a body of knowledge and skills that can improve the effectiveness of their work. However, the book also provides a common language to enable academic researchers to develop a productive dialogue with the aviation community. Such exchange of ideas will be beneficial for all, and will lead to an increase in cooperative human factors research involving academic and operational personnel. The authors are uniquely placed to write this book as they are based in a university that has successfully integrated operational flight training within an academic environment.

I am certain that this book will provide a valuable contribution to the intellectual resources, not only of the Bureau of Air Safety Investigation, but also to many other organisations throughout the aviation industry. I hope that the principles outlined will be applied, and thus contribute materially to safe and productive aviation operations throughout the world.

Dr Robert Lee
Director
Bureau of Air Safety Investigation.

List of Abbreviations

AAIB	Aircraft Accidents Investigation Branch
ANOVA	Analysis of Variance
APA	American Psychological Association
AOPA	Aircraft Owners and Pilots Association
ASRS	Aviation Safety Reporting System
BASI	Bureau of Air Safety Investigation
CAIR	Confidential Aviation Incident Reporting System
CASA	Civil Aviation Safety Authority
CBTD	Computer-Based Training Device
CGA	Conceptual Graph Analysis
CHIRP	Confidential Human Factors Incident Reporting Program
CRM	Crew Resource Management
CTA	Cognitive Task Analysis
df	Degrees of Freedom
EAA	Experimental Aircraft Association
FAA	Federal Aviation Administration
FDA	Food and Drug Administration
FGC	Fire Ground Commanders
FSF	Flight Safety Foundation
ICAO	International Civil Aviation Organization
ILS	Instrument Landing System
IMC	Instrument Meteorological Conditions
IQ	Intelligence Quotient
ISASI	International Society of Air Safety Investigators
LAME	Licensed Aircraft Maintenance Engineer
LED	Light-Emitting Diode
MANOVA	Multivariate Analysis of Variance
MBTI	Myers-Briggs Type Indicator
METAR	Meteorological Report
NASA	National Aeronautics and Space Administration
NHMRC	National Health and Medical Research Council
NTIS	National Technical Information Service

NTSB   National Transportation Safety Board
QAR   Quick Access Recorder
SME   Subject Matter Expert
SPSS   Statistical Package for the Social Sciences
TAF   Terminal Area Forecast
TSB   Transportation Safety Board of Canada
VFR   Visual Flight Rules
VMIQ   Vividness of Visual Imagery Movement Questionnaire
VVIQ   Vividness of Visual Imagery Questionnaire
WWW   World-Wide Web

1 Introduction

Ranging from the interpretation of accident/incident statistics at one extreme through to the evaluation of the outcomes of training initiatives at the other, 'research' offers a framework for effective decision-making and planning within complex industrial environments. Research provides the means for assessing market share, evaluating safety levels, projecting client demands, and/or identifying system failures. Consequently, the principles of research form an integral part of the successful management and maintenance of systems within the operational aviation environment.

Consistent with this perspective, the value of research within the operational environment is often evaluated on the basis of its outcomes, such as improved productivity or performance, and a consequent reduction in expenditure. Furthermore, the payoffs associated with research outcomes are expected to occur within a relatively short time frame, with as little investment as possible.

However, despite the desire for a structured, outcome-driven approach to the research process, the reality is considerably more complex, and it is often difficult to evaluate the product of research in purely economic terms. For example, the observers of the Wright brothers' initial flights found it particularly difficult to imagine the broader application of such an invention (McFarland, 1953). Indeed, as late as 1910, the brothers continued to experience a number of problems convincing the mainstream community of the value of aircraft (McFarland, 1953). This type of response exemplifies the need to consider research as a long-term investment that has the potential to yield significant outcomes, rather than as a 'single shot' attempt to solve complex problems.

Although 'single shot' research is attractive from an economic perspective, it should be noted that by far the greatest advances in modern science have generally occurred through a relatively systematic, cumulative approach to problem-solving. Typically, this involves an element of trial and error or 'educated' guesses such that particular avenues of thought are investigated and either pursued or disregarded depending upon the outcomes. This provides the basis for the development of a body of knowledge that, in turn, enables the development of effective and efficient solutions. Research into the causes of smallpox is an example of this type of research, where a number of approaches were investigated, some of which held promise, while others were disregarded as ineffective. However, the cumulative body of research provided a basis for understanding the nature and spread of smallpox and, therefore, facilitated the development of effective measures of eradication (Rains, 1974).

Aviation research is typical of most domains in which the progression of research outcomes has been characterised by initial, significant breakthroughs, followed by somewhat less significant refinements of existing knowledge. For example, although the Wright Flyer represented a particularly significant advance in the development of fixed-wing aviation, the components that constitute the design of more contemporary aircraft remain relatively consistent with the fundamental components that enabled the Wright Flyer to take to the air. This 'building block' approach to research is consistent with the history of research in other domains including medicine and biology, and is reflected in the saying 'we know more and more about less and less'. As a result, it is important to place the outcome of an individual research project in perspective, and consider it as part of a progression of research outcomes, rather than seek a panacea for all of the ills that confront a complex domain such as aviation.

The development of reasonable expectations is a significant part of the research process, although it is a lesson that is often learnt through painful experience. New researchers, in particular, tend to approach a project with the expectation that the outcomes will effect substantial changes within an area of study, either in terms of the acquisition of knowledge, or through the advancement of systems or technology. Typically, this expectation is directly proportional to the amount of time and energy invested in the project. However, for every scientist who has a place in history, there are many others whose effort and commitment to the research process were no less impressive. The difference lies both in the 'accidents' of history and the ability to capitalise upon those 'accidents' that do occur.

The relative value of a particular research study can be difficult to gauge, particularly during the early stages of the research process. Indeed, there have been dozens of cases throughout history in which researchers have posited theoretical positions that were considered impossible at the time. As early as 1694, Galileo supported the then heretical notion proposed by Copernicus that the earth revolved around the sun (Drake, 1957). Considered ludicrous at the time, Galileo and Copernicus were ultimately proven accurate, and this theoretical perspective altered both the nature of astronomy, and the philosophical perception of the place of humanity within the universe.

One of the most significant features associated with Galileo's research was the extent to which it impacted upon at least two relatively distinct research disciplines: astronomy and philosophy. However, the application of a single research outcome to more than one discipline is not a characteristic that is unique to Galileo. As an example, much of the aviation-related knowledge developed to ensure the destruction of the Axis powers during World War II was used subsequently as the basis for advances within civilian aviation. Similarly, the developments that have occurred within the commercial airline environment have provided the basis for improvements within general aviation.

The transfer of research outcomes between domains has also been evident in the development of training initiatives, particularly those associated with crew resource management. Helmreich and Davies (1997) noted that crew resource management initiatives, originally proposed for the aviation environment, have now been applied within domains as diverse as medicine and mining. Moreover, the principles of CRM are such that they have application to any complex domain where individuals are required to function as a team.

Despite the apparent ease with which research outcomes within one domain appear to be transferable to another, it is a strategy that is dependent upon an understanding of both the nature of the domain and the opportunities and limitations afforded by the research process. This book introduces readers to the process of research as it applies to human performance in the aviation environment. Furthermore, it outlines some of the assumptions associated with the research process in general and, more particularly, explores a number of different types of research paradigms. This aim of the book is to provide a foundation for systematic evaluations of aviation-related human performance, based upon sound methodological principles. To this end, the book provides a combination of both theoretical principles and practical guidelines to assist in the development, conduct and evaluation of research within an aviation context.

The structure of *Aviation Social Science: Research Methods in Practice* parallels the research process, beginning with the identification of an appropriate research problem. Although it may appear a relatively elementary task, the development of an appropriate research question can be one of the most difficult issues to confront the researcher. Therefore, Chapter 2 includes a list of potential text and web-based sources of information that will assist the development of aviation-related research questions. In addition, Chapter 2 discusses the principles of theory development as they apply to human performance research in aviation. Finally, the chapter includes an introduction to the characteristics and the generation of research questions and hypotheses.

Once an appropriate research question has been identified, the researcher is faced with an important decision concerning the type of investigative strategy that might be employed. In particular, there are a number of different approaches to research within the aviation environment including field observation, critical incident analysis, and task analysis. Each method has advantages and disadvantages, depending upon the particular circumstances within which it is applied. Chapter 3 explores a number of these approaches in some detail, and discusses their merits and pitfalls. In addition, a number of examples are described that illustrate the application of general research principles to particular aspects of the aviation environment.

Ultimately, the selection of a specific research strategy will involve a balance between a number of competing demands, including the requirement to adhere to appropriate ethical principles. An ethical approach to research ensures that potential participants are safeguarded from any harm that may emerge as part of the research process. Chapter 4 considers not only the nature of this relationship as it applies to the aviation environment, but also outlines a number of examples to illustrate the potential ethical dilemmas that can emerge for any researcher. Finally, guidelines are provided to facilitate the development and application of research strategies within an appropriate ethical context. Combined with the information provided in previous chapters, these guidelines establish the basis for the development of a research proposal.

The value in developing a research proposal is often overlooked, despite the fact that it offers an opportunity to consider, at the outset, the multitude of factors that are likely to impact upon the success of a particular research endeavour. These factors may include political issues, costs associated with the research process, the potential for methodological errors, and/or the potential for errors associated with the analysis of data. Chapter 5 examines both the role of the research proposal, and some of the mechanisms whereby these factors may be taken into account. It is designed to provide a practical approach that anticipates the conduct or process of research.

Throughout the book, there is an emphasis on the everyday, applied issues associated with the research process. This involves dealing with the various aspects of the aviation industry that are likely to be critical to the outcomes of the research. Aviation, like many other commercial industries, considers research as it does any other investment. There are costs associated with the acquisition of data, the outcomes of which may not yield sufficient benefits to the organisation. Therefore, an important part of the process of research involves the development of clear and concise arguments associated with the cost-benefits of research within the aviation environment. Chapter 6 considers the practical issues associated with conducting research and provides some guidelines to assist in obtaining a favourable outcome. However, it should be recognised that there are particular idiosyncrasies associated with the aviation system that may impact upon the quality of the research outcome, irrespective of the time and the investment made during the research planning phase. Ultimately, this is both the attraction and the risk associated with research in any applied environment.

Another part of research planning involves a consideration of the type of information or data that might be acquired, together with the techniques of data acquisition. A significant issue to face the researcher is whether the data will be quantitative, such as test scores, or qualitative, such as open-ended responses, or a combination of both. This will determine the types of data analytic procedures that may be applied. Chapter 7 is designed to introduce some of the issues involved in the analysis of research data. In particular, the notions of validity and reliability are examined, and a number of principles of data analysis are considered. This chapter provides a foundation for Chapters 8 and 9 that discuss inferential and qualitative data analytic techniques. These latter chapters have been designed to provide an introduction to the principles of data analysis, rather than a definitive account of the various procedures that might be applied. As there are comprehensive textbooks available regarding these techniques, readers are referred to useful resources in the area.

The penultimate chapter is designed to consider the publication of research outcomes. It is motivated by the view that researchers have a responsibility to publish the outcomes of research and contribute to the knowledge base within a particular area. In some cases, the publication of the outcomes of research will be more or less applicable to particular audiences. Therefore, the chapter considers the process of publishing in academic journals and in industry-based publications. Clearly, the audience for the two types of publications will be quite different, and the style of writing may reflect those differences. However, irrespective of the approach, the publication of sound research findings can meet the needs of both researchers and the operational personnel for whom the research may have been undertaken.

Given the expansion of the aviation industry and the demands for productivity and safety improvements, there is a growing need for human performance research within this complex and fascinating environment. *Aviation Social Science: Research Methods in Practice* is designed to introduce readers to aviation-related research and to stimulate their interest in the research process. To this end, all of the concepts, technical terms and research strategies that are discussed are related to the aviation environment. Furthermore, examples are used throughout the text to provide a concrete basis for the acquisition of knowledge and practical skills in the planning, conduct, and analysis of aviation-related research. One experimental example recurs throughout the text, presented in an information box. Important concepts are illustrated using this ongoing experimental theme.

Aviation Social Science: Research Methods in Practice is structured to mirror the research process. Despite its modular format, an effective method to grasp the concepts and ideas is to read through the material sequentially, as the later chapters tend to build upon concepts discussed earlier. A glossary of terms is provided towards the back of the book.

There is no need to possess an academic background to be effective as a researcher. Rather, research requires an inquiring mind, a passion for knowledge, and an organised and pragmatic approach to getting things done. These are elements that have characterised some of the most famous researchers throughout history, from Plato to Copernicus to Edison. *Aviation Social Science: Research Methods in Practice* is designed to develop fundamental research skills. Moreover, it provides a sound foundation for new researchers to investigate various aspects of the aviation environment with the confidence that they are using appropriate methods and techniques.

2 Identifying a Research Problem in Aviation

2.1 Introduction

Isolating a research problem within the aviation environment is not an easy task. First, novice researchers often find it difficult to know where to start isolating or defining a problem. Second, the success or otherwise of a research project is typically dependent upon the cooperation of an organisation that may or may not be comfortable with the research process. Finally, while it may be possible to solicit the cooperation of an aviation-based organisation, gaining the cooperation of potential participants is another matter entirely. Each of these factors contributes, at some level, to the difficulties faced by researchers during the process of scientific enquiry.

While acknowledging the difficulties associated with isolating research problems within the aviation environment, it is also important to acknowledge the significance that research plays, both in achieving changes within society, and in facilitating the development of safety-oriented initiatives.

This chapter considers the process of problem identification within the applied aviation environment. It begins with an analysis of the ways in which a problem can be identified and defined. The chapter then considers the nature of the scientific method and the distinction between basic and more applied research. This leads to a consideration of the 'research question' and the various types of questions that are employed within social science. A significant part of the problem-identification process is the review and analysis of relevant literature and the subsequent development of a particular theoretical perspective. The chapter concludes with an examination of the philosophical basis of both hypothesis generation and testing, and grounded theory, i.e. the description and subsequent analysis of phenomena as seen by those within the milieu.

2.2   The Nature of Social Scientific Research

Social science is a form of inquiry that falls somewhere between pure science at one extreme, and philosophical science at the other. Essentially, it involves the application of the scientific method as a means of understanding and/or predicting the characteristics associated with various human and social phenomena. Some of the areas of interest include communication, decision-making, information processing, human error, skill acquisition, group behaviour and leadership.

Social science incorporates a broad range of disciplines including history, psychology, education, anthropology, and sociology. Within these disciplines, the nature of research can range from highly controlled experiments through to surveys, questionnaires, individual case studies, to purely theoretical analyses and explanations. For example, experimental research refers to a process of inquiry whereby the impact of one variable is examined in the context of its influence upon another variable/s (Kerlinger, 1992). By contrast, more non-experimental accounts of behaviour, possibly based on qualitative information such as open-ended comments or survey responses, may seek to establish an understanding of the complexity and the diversity of social phenomena (Miles & Huberman, 1994).

Irrespective of the particular nature of inquiry, the characteristics of human and social phenomena are such that they are highly variable and difficult to control from an experimental perspective. For instance, human behaviour is likely to differ from flight to flight depending upon a number of factors including temperament, ability, and motivation. In contrast, the behaviour of a single chemical element will tend to remain relatively consistent.

In the aviation environment, social science research has been engaged in a number of areas including the nature of human error (O'Hare, Wiggins, Batt, & Morrison, 1994), crew resource management (Gregorich, Helmreich, & Wilhelm, 1990), personality selection (Burke, Hobson, & Linsky, 1997), flight instructor training (Henley, 1995), and the evaluation of training initiatives (Fisk & Gallini, 1989). The continued interest in the social scientific endeavour stems, in part, from the recognition that human error continues to account for a significant proportion of aircraft accidents and incidents (O'Hare et al., 1994; Ungs, 1994).

As in most industrial environments, successful social science research initiatives in aviation are dependent upon a cooperative arrangement between practitioners and researchers. The most important elements in this relationship are trust and communication. In many cases, the practitioner is in a particularly vulnerable position, and any breach of trust on the part of the researcher will have a significant impact upon the research outcomes.

2.2.1 The Scientific Method

According to Monette, Sullivan and DeJong (1986), the term 'research' is used to describe a variety of strategies of information acquisition from a student reading through a library catalogue to a police officer investigating the factors that may have been involved in a crime. However, in the social sciences, the term 'research' refers to a more specific form of inquiry involving 'the systematic examination (or re-examination) of empirical data collected by someone firsthand, concerning the forces operating in a situation' (Monette et al., 1986, p. 3).

Clearly, the most important implication of this definition is that social scientific research involves a process of systematic inquiry. The systematic nature of this type of information acqustion and analysis is the basis for what is referred to as the 'scientific method' or 'research process' (Monette et al., 1986). According to McGuigan (1997), this process involves:

1. The identification of a problem;
2. The development of a hypothesis or research question based upon previous research;
3. The collection of data in response to the hypothesis or research question;
4. A test of the data in respect of the hypothesis or research question;
5. A conclusion that refers to the initial problem;
6. The generalisation of findings, if appropriate, to other situations or phenomena; and
7. A consideration of the implications of the research outcomes in terms of general theory (adapted from McGuigan, 1997).

It is important to note that the research process is a general formulation of stages, rather than a step-by-step approach that prescribes the research process. Consequently, the strategies involved in achieving these stages can, and do, vary considerably.

Fundamentally, research incorporates a circuitous process in which the outcomes provide additional information concerning the initial research problem. In many cases, this will yield additional research problems that may be investigated subsequently. The culmination is a systematic process of information acquisition that contributes to a broader knowledge base, and yields a better understanding of a particular phenomenon.

2.2.2   Basic versus Applied Research

Like many other commercial endeavours, the aviation industry is facing a number of challenges of a social science nature, each of which has the potential to impact significantly upon the overall performance of the industry. For example, in the flight training environment, there is a strong emphasis on the development of more efficient and effective training initiatives (Anderson, 1993; Wiggins, Henley, Foley, & Moore, 1996; Smith, 1995).

Within the general aviation and airline industries, the emphasis is based upon such issues as fatigue (Petrie & Dawson, 1997), the management of passengers, and broader concerns such as occupational health and safety guidelines (Nakagawara & Wood, 1996). This is a reflection of the commercial reality faced by the aviation industry. Understandably, there is an emphasis on research outcomes that have the potential to deal with 'real-world' problems (Hedrick, Bickman, & Rog, 1993). This is the nature of *applied research.*

Applied research is often a compromise between strict adherence to the principles of experimentation and the requirement for timely research outcomes. This compromise is especially prevalent within the aviation domain where research can be relatively costly. In a number of cases, research outcomes have been published with fewer participants than might have been desirable from a purely experimental perspective (Braune, Stokes, & Wickens, 1985; Carmigniani & Palayret, 1989). These types of studies are generally referred to as *exploratory analyses*, and they can provide the basis for more detailed examinations in the future.

In contrast to applied research, basic research is concerned with the development of an understanding of fundamental structures or processes (Hedrick et al. 1993). In the human sciences, it might involve a strategy to understand the process by which visual information in the environment becomes neural activity in the brain. Therefore, basic research is designed to expand universal knowledge, and is almost exclusively a product of experimental research.

One of the main characteristics of basic research is the specificity of the research question. This is consistent with the notion of 'reductionism' in which the aim is to identify relationships within a highly controlled experimental environment. By exercising a high level of control, the researcher can ensure that the results obtained are not due to the impact of extraneous factors. For example, Perrott, Cisneros, McKinley, and D'Angelo (1996) used a laboratory environment to determine the extent to which the location and identification of a visual target could be aided through auditory or visual cues. Each participant was tested under six conditions: an unaided search condition; three aurally aided search conditions; and two visually aided search conditions. During all but the unaided search, an aural or visual cue would indicate to the participant the location of a target within a 4.3 metre sphere.

Each visual target consisted of a number of Light Emitting Diodes (LEDs), and participants were asked to count the number of LEDs and indicate, via left and right buttons, whether the number of LEDs was odd or even. The results indicated that auditory cues were most effective in terms of reducing the response time necessary to locate and identify a visual target from a previous line of gaze. Moreover, the distinction between visual and auditory cues was most pronounced for targets in the lower hemisphere of the display.

According to Perrott et al. (1996), these results provide the basis for a universal understanding of the interaction between the auditory and visual systems in humans. This research is indicative of a basic research paradigm, in which the outcomes can be generalised across a number of domains including aviation, air traffic control, and maritime operations. The ability to generalise results in this way is one of the most significant benefits associated with basic research (Banaji & Crowder, 1989).

Both basic and applied research paradigms have an important part to play in social scientific research. However, each is designed to fulfil different objectives, and the advantages and disadvantages of the two approaches are summarised in Table 2.1.

Table 2.1   A summary of advantages and disadvantages associated with the basic and applied research paradigms

	Advantages	Disadvantages
Basic Research	Experimental Control	Limited Application
	Universal Understanding	Specificity of the
	Time Required	Research Question
Applied Research	Applied Results	Lack of Control
	Multidisciplinary	Time Constraints
		Financial Constraints

2.3   Recognising a Research Problem

Choosing an appropriate research problem is the most important determinant for successful research. In the aviation environment, the research problem may be derived from a number of sources including personal experience, an analysis of accident or incident statistics, discussion with practitioners, or a critical review of the literature. However, irrespective of the mechanisms, the main requirements of a research question are that it lends itself to investigation, has the capacity to hold the interest of the researcher, and is relevant to the domain under investigation.

2.3.1   Personal Experience

In situations where a research problem is drawn from personal experience, some degree of caution needs to be exercised, particularly in terms of the acquisition and interpretation of the data. As within any profession, an excessive personal involvement in the problem may result in a level of bias in terms of the interpretation of data and the willingness to accept constructive criticism.

However, a level of personal experience does enable the researcher to identify and isolate factors that may otherwise be overlooked during the process of data analysis and interpretation. Similarly, personal experience may facilitate the development of more appropriate stimuli than might otherwise be the case, while personal contacts may be used to gain access to potential participants.

Box 2.1

An example of a research problem

As an example of a research question, let us consider the assumption that small amounts of blood alcohol impede pilot performance in the aviation environment. This is a widely held notion and likely to be uncontroversial. However, imagine that you have been asked to design a study to demonstrate that this is the case. In addition to the ethical principles we must adhere to in conducting our research (see Chapter 4), what form could the study take? How will we select participants for the study? What other factors or variables might need to be considered in the design and analysis of the study? How can we measure 'performance'? Will the study be conducted as a simulated task in the controlled conditions of a laboratory or conducted in a real-world, applied setting? What are the advantages and disadvantages of each approach?

As you will see, each step of the research design process requires the selection of specific conditions from a range of possibilities. These conditions relate to the who, what, where, when and how of the research study: who are the participants; what will the task be; where will it be conducted; when will the task be conducted and how will performance be measured accurately? Most importantly, we need to be able to justify why each of the conditions has been chosen over other possibilities.

2.3.2 *Aircraft Accident and Incident Analysis*

The data arising from aircraft accidents and incidents are outcome-driven, and such incidents are, therefore, well-recognised sources of research problems. Typically, summary sources are issued by government agencies on an annual basis and these are designed to categorise aircraft accidents on the basis of the factors involved in the occurrence. However, it should be noted that many accidents and incidents included in these summaries may not be subject to an independent investigation of the factors involved. Aircraft accident authorities are increasingly reliant upon pilots submitting aircraft accident and incident reports, and providing an explanation of the factors involved in these occurrences. While this approach may have some financial merit, the implication is that both individual reports and summary statistics need to be interpreted with some caution.

Most research involving human participants is conducted on a *random sample* of participants selected from a larger *population*. For example, a sample of 30 pilots may be tested from a total population of 2,000, since it is impractical to involve all members of a population in the study. Data analysis techniques are based on extrapolating the information from a sample to the larger population. In the case of aircraft accidents and incidents, the data are 'post-hoc': That is, the analysis is undertaken after the event has taken place. Therefore, the researcher had no direct control over the events and a number of variables (facts) may not have been known. As a consequence, it is very difficult to draw broad-based conclusions based on accidents or incidents, since the data do not necessarily constitute a representative sample of the wider population.

Confidential incident reporting systems such as the Aviation Safety Reporting System (ASRS), the Confidential Aviation Incident Reporting System (CAIR), and the Confidential Human Factors Incident Reporting Program (CHIRP) are also faced with the difficulty that the data obtained do not necessarily reflect a random sample of responses. Nevertheless, this type of information may provide a basis from which additional analyses can be undertaken. For example Billings and Reynard (1984) have provided a useful baseline of the human factors-related issues that emerged from ASRS data over a seven-year period. Any change in the relative proportion of factors within this type of data might be indicative of a research problem that requires additional analysis.

2.3.3   Discussion with Practitioners

In cases where the researcher is not familiar with the particular area of study, it is useful to engage in a dialogue with practitioners to determine precisely the nature of the problems that are evident within the workplace. The level of detail required will be dependent upon the nature of the research and the willingness of the practitioners to communicate their concerns.

Similarly, the process of information acquisition will be dependent upon the nature of the information required and can range from informal discussions to a formal process involving a task analysis. The latter is designed to provide a relatively systematic approach to the process of information acquisition and has the advantage of accommodating some level of objectivity (see Chapter 3: Section 3.4.4).

Taking the time to learn about the operational environment is an important part of applied research in the aviation environment. One of the most significant benefits is the opportunity to develop a research methodology with which potential participants can identify. Where the methodology is relatively abstract and/or appears to have little direct benefit for practitioners, the extent to which participants are likely to be involved is reduced. However, this approach needs to be tempered by the requirement for a rigorous research methodology that has the potential to closely examine a particular research problem.

2.3.4 Literature Review

Although the literature review is an essential aspect of the research process itself, it also provides a useful source of potential research problems. Some of the sources that should be considered as part of the literature review include technical reports, industry journals, books and academic journals: Some suggestions are made later in the chapter. Generally, research articles that are published in academic journals will include a consideration for future research within the area. This enables researchers to capitalise upon the research perspectives of more experienced researchers in the field.

Initially, the identification of a research problem through a literature review involves a relatively broad reading base in which the researcher will canvass a number of different areas of interest. Eventually, one or two research questions will emerge as a product of this process of filtering and analysis.

2.4 Characteristics of a Research Question

Research problems provide the basis for the development of a research question. Other than holding the interest of a particular researcher, a research question within the aviation domain should be relatively specific, have the potential to yield outcomes, and involve a cost effective and achievable methodology. Often, researchers may be tempted to examine a research question that is too broad to be examined successfully using a single methodological approach.

For example, determining the level of safety within a particular airline might incorporate a number of factors including attitudes towards safety, the frequency of incidents and accidents, the system health and/or the level of resources invested in the development and maintenance of safety practices. Each of these elements may constitute a single research question and, therefore, it may be necessary to establish research priorities, rather than attempt to examine each question simultaneously.

Research questions normally provide the basis for the development of the *research aim*. For example, the research question:

> 'What is the relationship between rostering practices and the incidence of occupational accidents amongst flight attendants?'

might be rephrased as a research aim to:

> 'The aim of this research study is to determine the relationship between rostering practices and the incidence of occupational accidents amongst flight attendants'.

Implicit within this statement is the research question, although it is the aim that is included as part of the subsequent research report.

2.5   Levels of Analysis

Throughout the process of research, there is a need to consider the level of analysis appropriate to the research question. The reductionist approach mentioned earlier conforms to the notion that complex phenomena must be 'reduced' to their constituents to enable valid and reliable comparisons to be made. Perhaps the clearest example of this strategy involves psychophysiological research where single cells are stimulated to determine their role in low-level visual perception. Clearly, the difficulty associated with this approach is the extent to which it neglects other factors such as personality, previous experience, or temperament. In the social sciences, these factors contribute significantly to the observed behaviour, and the particular data obtained.

While a reductionist approach is more characteristic of basic research paradigms, the systems approach is more evident in applied research, since behaviour is observed in the context of a number of factors, none of which is necessarily influenced by the researcher. Field research is an example of a systems approach where observations are made within the context of the operational environment. As a consequence of the variability that is likely to occur, there is no opportunity for the researcher to determine precisely the impact of one factor on another. Nevertheless, the systems approach has the advantage of taking into account the complexity of human behaviour.

The reductionist and systems approaches have significant implications for the specificity of the research question. In particular, where there is a dearth of previous research within a particular area, it may be necessary to adopt a relatively broad research question initially, as a transition to the development of more specific questions.

2.6   Types of Research Questions

Applied research questions can be divided according to the type of information required. For example, the question 'what are the characteristics of pilots who suffer from test anxiety?' is *descriptive*, while 'Is there a relationship between Intelligence Quotient (IQ) scores and pilot proficiency?' might be regarded as a *correlative* question (Hedrick et al. 1993). In the case of the latter, an association is posited, while the former seeks information to describe a particular population.

Where a comparison is made against a standard, the research question is referred to as *normative* (Hedrick et al. 1993). For example, the question 'do maintenance engineers in a particular airline adhere to the regulatory requirements at all times?' requires a comparison between the behaviour of the maintenance engineers against a standard: In this case, adherence to regulations.

In situations where a causal relationship is proposed, an *impact* research question is usually employed. As the term suggests, the researcher seeks information concerning the relative impact of one factor upon another. 'Does attendance at a Crew Resource Management (CRM) course increase the quality of verbal communication between aircrew?' is an example of this type of research question. Additional examples of the various types of research questions can be found in Table 2.2.

Table 2.2   Examples of the various types of research questions that are employed in applied social scientific research

Descriptive	What proportion of flight attendants experience significant life stressors associated with being away from home?
	How prevalent is alcohol abuse amongst international pilots?
	What are the traits that characterise expert air traffic controllers?
Correlative	Does a relationship exist between personality and ability to perform effectively as a pilot?
	Is there a relationship between spatial ability and performance as an air traffic controller?
Normative	Do Australian aviation qualifications meet the International Civil Aviation Organization (ICAO) guidelines?
	How serious is the aviation safety situation in developing nations?
Impact	Does a tertiary qualification increase the productivity of an employee within the aviation environment?
	Does attendance at a human factors course reduce the probability of being involved in a human factors-related accident/ incident?

Source: Adapted from Hedrick et al. (1993, p. 25).

2.7   Conducting a Literature Review

Having identified a research question, it is necessary to conduct a thorough search of the relevant literature in the area. This provides an important basis for the research as it facilitates the development of a theoretical perspective.

Irrespective of the particular type of research being conducted, a research study will generally involve some expectation of the outcome. This expectation may be the product of personal experience, observation or previous research. This understanding of the research domain is tantamount to a theoretical perspective, and it is from this conceptual basis that the researcher is conducting the study.

Social scientific research within the aviation domain is such that it would be extremely rare to conduct a piece of research for which there is no previous literature. While there may be a dearth of research concerning the particular area under investigation, it behoves the researcher to contemplate investigating allied research areas to assist with the development of a theoretical perspective. For example, an investigation of the rate of skill acquisition during a flight training sequence could incorporate a consideration of similar research that may have been conducted in other fields such as chess, medicine, or racquet ball. Generally, a number of principles are likely to emerge that will facilitate the investigation into flight training. These principles may include methodological issues, strategies for data analysis, and/or suggestions for future research initiatives.

2.7.1   Conducting a Literature Search

Clearly, the extent of the literature search in a particular domain will be dependent upon the type of research being contemplated and the resources available to the researcher. For example, the acquisition of resources can be costly if the material needs to be procured from an overseas source. Consequently, the benefits associated with the acquisition of this material need to be weighed against the costs involved.

Most libraries (including public libraries) have the capacity to locate and acquire resources from libraries throughout the world. The difficulty for the researcher involves the location of relevant material, and the time required to retrieve this material. For example, in the social sciences, the range of journals and texts is particularly diverse, and there is often no single resource to which researchers can refer to locate relevant research.

In the psychology and education-related domains there are databases available on CD-ROM that are updated regularly, and which are capable of searches by subject. These are known as PsycINFO and ERIC respectively, and they can be useful starting points for the literature search. Having identified a piece of relevant literature, the references in these articles can be used as the basis for subsequent literature searches. Another useful source of information is the World-Wide Web (WWW) search engine at the National Technical Information Service (NTIS). This is the central document store for most United States government publications (unclassified). Documents including National Transportation Safety Board Reports can be purchased from the NTIS.

The use of the WWW as an information source is becoming more and more widespread. A growing number of academic journals are now available on-line and include search and retrieve functions. Generally, access to these journals can be obtained by contacting a university library or the publishers of the journals. A wide variety of magazine and newspaper articles are also accessible on-line and the list of available publications is increasing. It should be noted that there may be costs involved in retrieving on-line information, as these publications would normally be available through a library for which a copyright royalty is paid. Nevertheless, accessing journals and magazines on-line can save a great deal of time.

An important part of the literature search is lateral thinking, such that a wide variety of potential resources are canvassed in an effort to source any relevant material. For example, if a particularly relevant and thorough article is found, the keywords, together with the author's name might be used to locate any other associated articles. A list of some of the potential academic resources available is provided in Table 2.3.

In addition to academic resources, non-academic publications can also provide useful information for the development of a theoretical perspective. Table 2.4 lists some of the resources that are available.

Table 2.3   Relevant academic journals for social science research in aviation

- The International Journal of Aviation Psychology
- Human Factors
- Journal of Experimental Psychology: Applied
- Journal of Experimental Psychology: Human Perception and Performance
- Cognitive Science
- Ergonomics
- Applied Ergonomics
- Journal of Aviation/Aerospace Education and Research
- Aviation, Space and Environmental Medicine
- Organisational Behaviour and Human Decision Processes
- *IEEE* Transactions on Systems, Man, and Cybernetics
- Office of Aviation Medicine, Federal Aviation Administration (FAA)
- Human Performance
- Applied Psychology: An International Review
- Educational Researcher
- Journal of Personality and Social Psychology
- Journal of Applied Psychology
- International Journal of Human-Machine Studies
- Journal of Applied Social Psychology
- Military Psychology
- Review of Educational Research
- Spatial Vision
- Human Factors in Transportation
- Journal of Safety Research
- Accident Analysis and Prevention

Table 2.4   Relevant non-academic journals for social science research in aviation

- International Society of Air Safety Investigators (ISASI) Forum
- National Transportation Safety Board (NTSB) Accident Reports
- Bureau of Air Safety Investigation (BASI) Accident and Incident Reports
- Air Accidents Investigation Branch (AAIB) Accident and Incident Reports
- Transportation Safety Board (TSB) Accident Reports
- Aircraft Owners and Pilots Association – Safety Reviews
- Kai Talk (Cathay Pacific Airways Safety Magazine)
- Asia-Pacific Air Safety Magazine
- Airliner (Boeing Safety and Product Information Magazine)
- Aviation Safety Review
- Flight Deck (British Airways Safety Magazine)
- Flight Safety (Singapore Airlines Safety Magazine)
- Flight Safety Digest (Flight Safety Foundation Publication)
- Feedback (Confidential Human Factors Incident Reporting Scheme)
- Callback (Aviation Safety Reporting System)
- Aerospace (Royal Aeronautical Society Magazine)
- Ergonomics in Design
- Air Line Pilot
- Business and Commercial Aviation
- International Civil Aviation Organization (ICAO) Journal
- Flight Training

The internet provides another valuable source of social scientific information in the aviation environment. The following homepages are useful sites:

www.arc.nasa.gov/	National Aeronautics and Space Administration (NASA)
www.faa.gov/	Federal Aviation Administration (FAA)
www.basi.gov.au/	Bureau of Air Safety Investigation (BASI)
www.ntsb.gov/	National Transportation Safety Board (NTSB)
www.bst-tsb.gc.ca/	Transportation Safety Board (TSB)
www.open.gov.uk/aaib/	Air Accidents Investigation Branch (AAIB)
www.flightsafety.org/	Flight Safety Foundation (FSF)
www.cam.org/~icao/	International Civil Aviation Organization (ICAO)
www.ntis.gov/	National Technical Information Service (NTIS)

It is also possible to use an internet browser or a search engine to search for safety-related information on the internet. In doing so, it is important to exercise some caution in relying upon the veracity of the material that is acquired. In many cases, material that is placed on the internet is neither reviewed nor edited. Therefore, the reader is unable to determine the accuracy or reliability of the information provided, unless the original source is located.

2.8   Position Papers versus Empirical Research

When conducting a literature review, it is important to note the distinction between position papers and those that involve empirical research. From an academic perspective, position papers are regarded as a synthesis of existing research within a particular domain that provides a statement of the current position of knowledge. This type of article is useful to the extent that it provides a summary of the empirical research that has been conducted within an area of study.

While there is certainly an important place for position papers within the academic environment, some degree of caution needs to be exercised when using position papers as the sole basis for a literature review. Position papers are subject to a level of interpretation and are regarded, like textbooks, as secondary sources. Normally, researchers would be expected to obtain the primary work from which the position was derived, rather than rely upon the interpretations of others.

2.9   Development of Theory

Part of the process of conducting a literature review is the development of a theoretical perspective regarding the relationship or differences between two or more variables. For example, Becker, Warm, Dember, and Hancock (1995) developed a potential research question concerning the relationship between intermittent jet aircraft noise and performance during a vigilance task. An analysis of the literature in the area revealed two competing theories about the relationship between noise and its impact upon performance.

The first of these theories postulates that there is no direct relationship between noise and a deterioration in human performance (Koelega & Brinkman, 1986). However, the second theory suggests that a systematic relationship exists, due to the increase in information processing load that noise imposes upon human behaviour. Becker et al. (1995) extended the latter theory to postulate that, since intermittent noise has an impact on information-processing, it should also have an impact upon perceptions of workload. This is an example of a theoretical perspective and it provides the basis for the deduction of a hypothesis that can be subjected to testing.

The status of scientific theory has been the subject of much debate by philosophers. Contrary to popular belief, scientific investigation and theorising does not yield immutable proven laws. On logical grounds, theories or hypotheses are never unquestionably true or proven. Chalmers (1988) summarises the situation as follows. 'Theories are construed as speculative and tentative conjectures...Once proposed, speculative theories are to be rigorously and ruthlessly tested by observation and experiment. Theories that fail to stand up to observational and/or experimental tests must be eliminated and replaced by further speculative conjectures. Science then progresses by trial and error, by conjectures and refutations. Only the fittest theories survive. While it can never be legitimately said of a theory that it is true, it can hopefully be said that it is the best available, that it is better than anything that has come before' (p. 38).

There is a general consensus that an important characteristic of a scientific theory and hypothesis is that it is falsifiable. Logically, it is not possible to prove beyond doubt that something *is* the case. However, it is possible to arrive at the falsity of theories and hypotheses by logical deduction. For example, the hypothesis that all ravens are black can be rejected if a raven that is not black is observed at a particular place and time. The notion of falsifiability rests on the assumption that science can progress not by proving that things *are* the case, but by performing logical deductions that are valid in the *negative* instance. A hypothesis is falsifiable if there exists a logically possible observation statement that is inconsistent with it. Hypotheses such as: (a) It never rains on Wednesdays; and (b) All substances expand when heated, are falsifiable. If it is possible to establish the truth of an observation statement that is inconsistent with it, then the hypothesis would be falsified. As an example, hypothesis (a) would be falsified by observing rain falling on Wednesdays. Therefore, a negative instance can disprove a hypothesis and, for this reason, the experimental method is sometimes described as a method of disproof (Chalmers, 1988).

In developing and testing hypotheses, the requirement of falsifiability should be met. In the case of the theory proposed by Becker et al. (1995), the proposed relationship between intermittent noise and workload would be false if, following testing, no relationship between the two measures was evident. On the other hand, if a relationship was evident between the two variables, then the researcher may conclude that the evidence has provided support for that theoretical perspective.

Despite the applied nature of research within the aviation environment, it is important to note that scientific inquiry is not designed specifically to yield applied outcomes. For example, Kerlinger (1992) contends that the aim of science and scientific inquiry is fundamentally the development and investigation of theory. This assertion is based upon the premise that science involves the explanation of phenomena, and that this explanation is, in effect, a theoretical perspective. Consequently, the notions of 'science' and 'theory' are inextricably linked.

The difficulty within the aviation environment is that applied outcomes are often developed in the absence of 'good' theory. This can lead to applied research that is less effective than might otherwise have been the case. As an example, consider an organisation in which a significant proportion of the population experiences backache due to poorly designed office furniture. From an applied perspective, the obvious solution is to 'fix' the furniture. *How* it might be fixed is another question. Unless the researcher/ designer possesses an accurate theory (understanding) of the ergonomic relationship between the human form and the furniture, then the problems are unlikely to be solved. This requires additional research at a more basic level of scientific inquiry. Although the results will not be directly applicable to the aviation environment, they can provide the basis for solutions to applied problems such as the back problems experienced by many pilots.

2.10   Hypothesis Generation

The process of conducting a literature review can be likened to a funnel into which a large amount of information and data are poured (see Figure 2.1). The product of this synthesis is a clear, concise statement of expectation, referred to as a *hypothesis*. In the earlier proposition concerning flight attendant rostering and occupational accidents, previous research in the area might lead to the theory that a relationship exists between particular rostering practices and the incidence of occupational accidents (see Section 2.4). Consequently, it might be hypothesised that a break of 15 hours between shifts results in fewer occupational accidents than a break of 12 hours between shifts.

From a scientific perspective, the hypothesis is a statement of position against which the results can be tested. It is specific to the research, and can be more or less complex depending upon the nature of the investigation. In some cases, a series of hypotheses may be necessary to take into account the complexity of a research study. This process of developing and testing a hypothesis that has been deduced from theory is referred to as the hypothetico-deductive method of scientific inquiry (Harré, Gundlach, Métraux, Ockwell, & Wilkes, 1985; Hull, 1943).

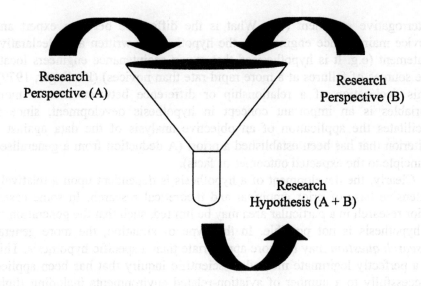

Research
Perspective (A)

Research
Perspective (B)

Research
Hypothesis (A + B)

Figure 2.1 An illustration of the process of conducting a literature review

A 'deductive' argument is one in which the conclusion is a logical and certain outcome of the premises. For example, Becker et al. (1995) propose the following premises concerning the relationship between intermittent noise, information processing, and workload.

1. High volume levels of intermittent noise have an adverse impact upon successful performance during vigilance tasks which require high levels of information processing;
2. Successful performance during a vigilance task is dependent upon the availability of sufficient attentional resources;
3. The availability of attentional resources is inversely proportional to the level of workload imposed (adapted from Becker et al., 1995).

On the basis of these premises, it can be deduced that *high volume levels of intermittent noise are directly related to perceptions of workload during those vigilance tasks which require high levels of information processing*. This becomes the basis for the *experimental hypothesis:* the hypothesis against which experimental evidence is sought.

The hypothesis is typically a progression from a broader research question or problem. However, where the research problem is an interrogative statement (e.g. What is the difference between expert and novice maintenance engineers?), the hypothesis is written as a declarative statement (e.g. It is hypothesised that expert maintenance engineers locate the sources of failures at a more rapid rate than novices) (Kerlinger, 1979). This declaration of a relationship or difference between two or more variables is an important concept in hypothesis development, since it facilitates the application of an objective analysis of the data against a criterion that has been established a priori (A deduction from a generalised principle to the expected outcomes or facts).

Clearly, the development of a hypothesis is dependent upon a relatively extensive base of prior empirical and theoretical research. In some cases, prior research in a particular area may be limited, such that the generation of a hypothesis is not possible. In this type of situation, the more general *research question* may be more appropriate than a specific hypothesis. This is a perfectly legitimate method of scientific inquiry that has been applied successfully to a number of aviation-related environments including flight instruction (Henley, 1991) and low-level fighter operations (Haber, 1987).

2.11   Testing the Hypothesis

There is a wealth of literature and debate concerning hypothesis testing, the nature of scientific enquiry, inductive versus deductive reasoning, the philosophy of science and the hypothetico-deductive method. Accounts of the broad issues and debates can be found in Barratt (1971), Chalmers (1988), Kuhn (1970), Feyerabend (1975), and Popper (1969): A list of suggested references can be found at the end of this chapter. The hypothetico-deductive method that has been sketched is a positivistic approach and one that is influenced by Popper's (1969) notion of falsifiability and the test of hypotheses deduced from theory.

Having specified a hypothesis, it is important to ensure that the approach taken during the process of testing remains consistent with the principle of falsifiability and deduction (Popper, 1969). Recall that this principle requires that the researcher identify the circumstances under which the hypothesis will be rendered false. The notion of falsifiability influences both the statement of hypotheses and their evaluation using statistical testing techniques (See Section 8.3).

Box 2.2

The development of a hypothesis

The design of our study on alcohol and pilot performance, and the hypothesis to be tested, will be based on previous and related studies and, perhaps, a theoretical framework. In general terms, we need to identify the factors or variables to be considered, the way they are to be manipulated and the way that the effects of the manipulation might be measured. For example, we might propose an experimental hypothesis that flying performance is poorer under conditions of moderate alcohol intake, relative to low and no alcohol intake for pilots of different ages.

We need to specify the levels of the variables to be manipulated, identify extraneous factors that may have an influence and, therefore, need to be controlled, and establish the task and index of performance. Specifically, we might have three levels of alcohol (none, low and moderate) and three levels of age (17-20 years; 21-24 years; 25-28 years). The task or test could be a simulation of flying in a real-world setting, a simulation in controlled laboratory conditions, or even computer-based tests of abilities used in flying, such as visual tracking or motion detection. An efficient technique would be to measure performance before and after the ingestion of alcohol, and use the difference between the two scores as an index of the effect of alcohol level on performance.

Now consider this study in light of the entries in Table 2.1 and the advantages and disadvantages of basic and applied research. A series of laboratory-based computer tasks (basic research) offers the greatest control of factors that relate to the individual participant, the stimuli, and the measurement of task performance. However, the results may or may not extrapolate to the operational environment. The simulation of flying involves the participants in a much more realistic context and task, although this is achieved at the expense of the control of many factors that may impact upon performance.

From a statistical point of view, the null hypothesis specifies the circumstances under which the experimental hypothesis is rendered false. The term 'null hypothesis' is used, since it often proposes that no difference or relationship will be evident between two or more variables. The result, in the case of Becker et al. (1995), is a null hypothesis that proposes no relationship between levels of intermittent noise and perceptions of workload. By contrast, the experimental hypothesis specifies a relationship between intermittent noise and the perception of workload.

Technically, pairs of hypotheses are normally constructed: The null hypothesis and the experimental, or alternative, hypothesis. With the notion of falsifiability in mind, the researcher gathers evidence and attempts to test the null hypothesis. By rejecting the null hypothesis, support is provided for the experimental hypothesis. However, if the results do not permit rejection of the null hypothesis, then there is no support for the experimental/alternative hypothesis.

At this stage, it is important to recall that hypotheses are an outcome of theory. Therefore, rejection of the null hypothesis provides implicit support for some aspect of the theory. However, as Chalmers (1988) notes, theories can never be accepted as true, despite the level of testing to which they may be subjected. A current theory can simply be regarded as superior, since it has been able to withstand tests that falsified alternative theories.

As mentioned, the principle of hypothesis testing has been the subject of considerable debate within the field of science, and Barratt (1971) observes that hypotheses are simply tools to enable a scientist to undertake the task of experimentation. Therefore, they should not be regarded as immutable formulae that are either true or false. Rather, hypotheses provide the basis for the accumulation of knowledge through progressive tests and the observation of consequences.

2.12   Chapter Summary

This chapter was designed to introduce some of the principles of social scientific research in the aviation environment. As is evident, it is important to consider a number of competing aspects, almost simultaneously, in order to minimise the impact of any problems that may occur during the later stages of the research.

One of the most important factors associated with the research process involves the selection of an appropriate research problem. In most cases, the research problem should hold some interest for the investigator and should provide for a cost-effective and efficient methodology.

The research problem provides the basis for the development of the research question, the specificity of which will be dependent upon the characteristics of the research being undertaken. This process should occur in conjunction with a detailed literature review such that the researcher has a substantial theoretical basis from which to develop hypotheses (see Figure 2.2). However, since the hypothesis is a statement of expectation, it is dependent upon a relatively extensive research base that may not be available in some domains. Consequently, a research question may be considered more appropriate than a hypothesis in some situations.

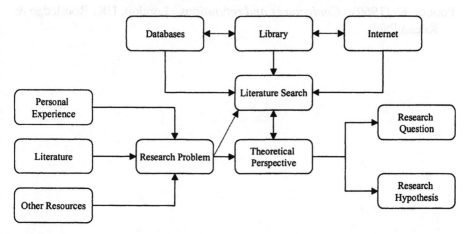

Figure 2.2   A summary of the process from identifying a research problem to developing a hypothesis

2.13   Further Reading

Barratt, P.E.H. (1971). *Bases of psychological methods.* Brisbane, AUS: Wiley.

Bell, P.B., & Staines, P.J. (1979). *Reasoning and argument in psychology.* Sydney, AUS: University of New South Wales Press.

Chalmers, A.F. (1988). *What is this thing called science?* (2nd Ed.). St. Lucia, AUS: University of Queensland Press.

Christensen, L.B. (1991). *Experimental methodology* (5th ed.). Boston, MA: Allyn & Bacon.

Dyer, C. (1995). *Beginning research in psychology.* Oxford, UK: Blackwell.

Feyerabend, P.K. (1975). *Aganist method: Outline of an anarchistic theory of knowledge.* London, UK: New Left Books.

Hempel, C.G. (1966). *Philosophy of natural science.* Englewood Cliffs, NJ: Prentice-Hall.

Kuhn, T.S. (1970). *The structure of scientific revolutions.* Chicago, IL: Chicago University Press.

Popper, K. (1969). *Conjectures and refutations.* London, UK: Routledge & Kegan Paul.

3 Social Science Research Strategies in Aviation

3.1 Introduction

As human behaviour is complex, studies of human behaviour are themselves likely to be complex. However, analyses of behaviour need not be complicated and some of the simplest research designs can often yield the most useful data. The optimal approach involves balancing the need for simplicity against the characteristics (variables) that might have an impact upon human performance.

The relative influence of individual variables may differ, and any effects of the interactions between these variables needs to be taken into account. This can create some difficulties for the researcher in terms of the resources required and the time available in which to conduct the study. This chapter considers the nature and structure of research design in the social sciences.

Chapter 3 also considers important principles associated with research design, including sampling techniques, counterbalancing, and the identification and minimisation of confounding factors. These key principles require a level of planning on the part of the researcher. By planning ahead, the researcher can anticipate the various outcomes and take the necessary steps to facilitate the acquisition of data that are accurate and reliable. There is nothing more disappointing than to reach the analysis phase and realise that a fundamental issue has been overlooked during the process of data acquisition.

3.2 Types of Research

Depending upon the particular domain under investigation, a researcher may apply one of a number of distinct approaches to the identification and analysis of a research problem (see Figure 3.1). These can range from single-participant case studies to surveys of a large sample of the population; from observations in the field to highly controlled, laboratory studies. Each type of research design has advantages and disadvantages and these issues need to be considered as part of the development of a particular research question. The various designs are discussed throughout the chapter.

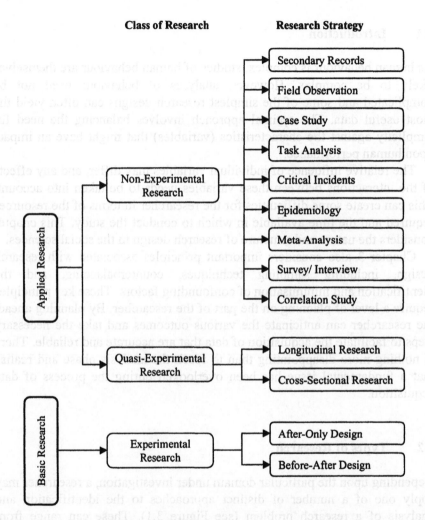

Figure 3.1   An illustration of the classes of social science research and some of the types of research strategies that fall within these classes

There are two main classes of research in the social sciences: non-experimental research and experimental research. A third class, quasi-experimental research, includes aspects of both non-experimental and experimental research. Non-experimental techniques form the basis of most research initiatives within the social sciences and include secondary research, case studies, field research, correlational studies, meta-analyses and surveys. In contrast, experimental and quasi-experimental paradigms are typically applied within an environment in which the variables can be manipulated and controlled.

Box 3.1

An appropriate class of research

Although our research question concerning alcohol and pilot performance is very much an applied and real-world issue, it would be impossible to conduct this study under everyday conditions. More likely, the study would make use of a flight simulator. However, it would also be possible to design a series of laboratory, computer-based tests that measure perceptual, motor, cognitive and reaction time skills. These tests could be controlled precisely in terms of difficulty, timing of presentation and instructions and could, thereby, meet the requirements for experimental research. Although they may not be explicit replicas of operational behaviour, they could be designed to tap the abilities used in flying. The results from such controlled settings can then be extrapolated to more 'real-world' tasks.

As an example, Macarthur and Sekuler (1982) conducted an experiment on the effect of blood alcohol levels on motion perception. The motion perception tasks involved judgements of direction, reaction time to movement, and direction uncertainty. Although the tests were not specific analyses of operational performance, the authors concluded that such tests could be useful for detecting performance with low blood alcohol levels.

3.3   Variables

A variable can be defined as any characteristic, the value of which can alter. For example, the age of a group of flight attendants can be regarded as a variable, since the ages of a random sample of flight attendants will vary. Similarly, pilots' susceptibility to test anxiety, and students' research writing skills can both be regarded as variables.

A research design generally involves the systematic manipulation and measurement of variables. The variables that are manipulated by the experimenter are referred to as independent variables. McGuigan (1997) defines an independent variable as 'an aspect of the environment that is empirically investigated for the purpose of determining whether it influences behaviour' (p.454). Independent variables can relate to characteristics of the participants such as age, years/hours flying experience, anxiety level (organismic variables) or to characteristics of stimuli such as task difficulty (stimulus variables).

An experiment consists of at least one independent variable and each variable has at least two levels. If flying experience was an independent variable, it might consist of two levels: 1,000-1,200 hours and 3,000-3,500 hours. Clearly, the independent variable could have more than these two levels, but there must be at least two. It would be impossible to draw any conclusions from a study wherein a variable contained only a single level. There would be very little to say about the effect of a small amount of flying experience, unless it is compared with the effect of a relatively greater amount of flying experience.

Independent variables can take many forms. Consider the range of variables that could be manipulated in the study of the effects of alcohol (see Box 3.1). Not only could the effects of different levels of alcohol be manipulated and measured, but the effect of organismic variables such as the age of the participant, experience, or gender could also be examined. Generally, a theoretical perspective motivates the choice of the independent variables that are to be manipulated. For example, there may be a theoretical basis or previous findings to suggest that gender and/or years flying experience has an effect on performance. There are limits to the number of independent variables that can be manipulated in a single study and it is not uncommon for two or three variables to be included. However, if there are a large number of levels associated with a particular independent variable, the total number of variables should be kept to a minimum.

The second kind of variable is termed the dependent variable and this refers to a measurable response or index of performance. More formally, McGuigan (1997) states that 'a dependent variable is a well-defined aspect of behaviour (a response) that is measured in a study. The value that the dependent variable assumes is hypothesized to be dependent on the value assumed by the independent variable so it is expected to be a change in behaviour that is related systematically to the independent variable...' (p. 450). The choice of a reliable and valid dependent variable is an important one and is influenced by the kind of task that is relevant and whether the setting for the study is to be laboratory-based or set within the operational environment. It is worth researching to determine whether there already exist reliable and valid instruments or measures available. In measuring flying performance, a number of variables could be measured including accuracy or the number of errors. A precise set of preplanned criteria would be required to ensure that the measurement of performance was constant across all participants and conditions. A useful technique is to measure pre-treatment and post-treatment performance. Participants then act as their own controls and the dependent measure is simply the difference in scored performance (either better or worse) after the administration of the experimental treatment.

Variables are typically identified through the process of developing a hypothesis or research question. The hypothesis is such that it will embody the variables under investigation. For example, it might be hypothesised that a relationship exists between the scores obtained on a computer anxiety inventory and the length of time taken to reach criterion performance using a computer program. In this case, the scores on the inventory and the time taken to reach criterion performance refer to the independent variable and the dependent variable that are under investigation, respectively.

Although the notion of 'variables' is normally associated with experimental research and quantitative data, variables do have a place in more qualitative research paradigms, although they tend to emerge during the course of the research. For example, Klein (1989) posed a general research question pertaining to the nature of the decision-making behaviour of Fire Ground Commanders (FGC) during critical situations. The study yielded a number of key results including the application of mental simulation and serial processing during the decision-making process. These variables have been targeted in subsequent research endeavours to improve aeronautical decision-making (Urban, Weaver, Bowers, & Rhodenizer, 1996).

3.3.1   Controlling Variables

Clearly, there may be many more relevant variables than can be manipulated within a study. Rather than manipulating and assessing the effect of all of the possible variables, these extraneous variables can be controlled. If it is likely that variables, such as the number of years flying experience, sex, body mass index, and/or task complexity, are likely to affect performance, it is possible to minimise their influence by ensuring that all the participants are approximately equal with respect to these factors. For example, a study might be conducted using only male participants who have a similar body mass index, similar experience, while the task will be of moderate complexity.

Therefore, it is important to be aware of the two meanings of 'control' in an experimental study. First, there are *control variables* to minimise the effect of extraneous factors on performance. By contrast, the second meaning of control refers to a *control group* where the participants receive some normal or standard or zero treatment condition. The performance of this group acts as the standard, against which the treatment administered to the experimental group(s) may be evaluated (McGuigan, 1997).

It should be noted that the assumption that two or more variables are related ignores the possibility that other variables may also impact upon a particular outcome. For example, the relationship that exists between age and increasing levels of expertise ignores the fact that with increasing age there is the possibility of a greater level of exposure to the operating environment and, therefore, a greater opportunity to develop the skills necessary for expertise. Consequently, it may be necessary to exercise some degree of control over variables to ensure that they do not confound the data.

In the case of the relationship between age and expertise, it may be necessary to ensure that each participant in a research study has had a similar opportunity to interact with the operating environment. This process is referred to as 'matching', and it is one mechanism whereby the influence of an extraneous variable (in this case exposure to the operating environment) can be controlled.

The notion of exercising control over variables is based upon the assumption that variables, other than those being examined, can impact upon the research results. Consequently, both non-experimental and experimental research designs require that researchers consider those variables that may influence the results and ensure that the impact of these variables is controlled.

3.4 Non-Experimental Research

Non-experimental research attempts to clarify the existence of phenomena, and/or the nature of relationships between aspects of phenomena (Mitchell & Jolley, 1992). A variety of strategies may be used, depending upon the level of intervention and the type of data required.

Since non-experimental research generally occurs within the operational environment, the experimenter often has very little control over the frequency and the nature of the events that occur. Therefore, non-experimental research is **not** designed to identify associations between 'cause' and 'effect'. The aim of non-experimental research is to provide a valid and reliable description. However, these results might be used subsequently as the basis for experimental or quasi-experimental research in which a greater level of control can be exercised.

An example of the complementary relationship between experimental and non-experimental research can be drawn from the extensive body of research involving the 'black hole' approach and landing. Research interest in this area arose from a series of aircraft accident reports which described commercial aircraft landing short of the runway during night approaches, despite the fact that the weather was clear and the runway was visible in the distance (Hull, Gill, & Roscoe, 1982; Roscoe, 1979; 1982).

In response to these reports, Kraft (1978) conducted a series of simulator-based, quasi-experimental analyses of visual approaches at night, and noted that during particular configurations, pilots would suffer from a visual illusion in which there was an appearance of excessive altitude. This would result in a premature descent which, unless arrested, could ultimately result in a collision with terrain.

According to Kraft (1978), the particular configurations during which the 'black hole' illusion occurred involved a long shallow approach over unlit terrain towards an illuminated airport in the distance. Clearly, this had significant operational implications, but it also led to a series of subsequent quasi-experimental and experimental studies to determine the features of the visual system through which this type of illusion occurred (Hull et al., 1982; Iavecchia, Iavecchia, & Roscoe, 1988; Roscoe, 1979; 1982; Meehan & Triggs, 1992; Smith, Meehan, & Day, 1992). This illustrates the type of relationship that often exists between non-experimental paradigms, in which a problem may be identified, and experimental research, wherein a problem is isolated and analysed.

3.4.1   Secondary Records

A number of researchers have employed *secondary records* as the basis of analyses within the aviation environment including Billings and Reynard (1984), O'Hare et al. (1994), Salvatore, Stearns, Huntley and Mengert (1986) and Shappell and Wiegmann (1997). In the case of Billings and Reynard (1984), the secondary records involved incident reports arising from the confidential Aviation Safety Reporting System (ASRS) database. O'Hare et al. (1994) and Shappell and Wiegmann (1997) used published aircraft accident and incident reports as the basis for their analyses, while Salvatore et al. (1986) were more reliant upon aircraft accident and incident statistics.

In general, the application of secondary records is subject to a great deal of interpretation and, therefore, a great deal of caution should be exercised when using this type of data as the basis for research. However, there are a number of mechanisms to ensure that the conclusions derived from secondary reports are as accurate as possible. One of the most important strategies involves the use of independent raters when there is a requirement to categorise or classify reports. This is designed to ensure that one person's interpretation of a report is relatively objective, and can be replicated.

In addition, it is important to use some form of theoretical structure to assist in the classification of reports. Both O'Hare et al. (1994) and Shappell and Wiegmann (1997) adopted theoretical models based upon the characteristics of human error. Essentially, the goal is either to test the extent to which a particular model can account for various aircraft accidents or incidents, or the extent to which particular types of errors are prevalent within a particular part of the aviation industry. The specific strategy used will be dependent upon the type of research question that is asked.

The use of secondary records is especially useful when a research domain is relatively ill-defined. It enables an area to be targeted for further analysis. For example, O'Hare et al. (1994) noted that a strong relationship existed between aircraft accidents arising from decision errors and the seriousness of the consequences in terms of the injuries sustained by the occupants of the aircraft. While it is not possible to assert that decision errors *cause* serious injuries, the relationship is, nevertheless, worthy of additional research.

The main disadvantage associated with the application of secondary sources is that the information is often subject to a great deal of interpretation, both by the reporter and by the experimenter. Consequently, the researcher is reliant upon the accuracy of data over which there is no direct control. This may result in ambiguous results that limits the extent to which they can be generalised.

3.4.2   Field Observation

As a means of overcoming some of the disadvantages associated with the reliance upon secondary reports, field observation provides the researcher with a greater level of control over the quality of the data acquired and, therefore, the nature of the research outcomes. However, this type of strategy involves a greater level of intervention than would otherwise be the case and this may have some impact upon the performance of the participants.

The main advantage associated with the application of field observation techniques is the opportunity to observe behaviour within the natural environment (Hedrick et al. 1993). This contrasts with more experimental, laboratory-based research techniques in which the research outcomes may not necessarily reflect behaviour that occurs within the more complex operational environment.

The most interventionist of the field observation techniques involves the researcher recording task performance in real-time. For example, in the case of aircrew, a researcher may occupy the jumpseat and may record data as the flight progresses (Bowers, Deaton, Oser, Prince, & Kolb, 1995). Although this technique has the advantage of providing an opportunity for the acquisition of information from a wide variety of sources, it may impact adversely upon the performance of the participants and, thereby, lead to erroneous results. This type of response is referred to as the 'audience effect'. Consequently, a great deal of caution needs to be exercised when recording information in real-time. Moreover, the researcher needs to have some consideration of the needs of the participants involved.

A relatively less interventionist approach may involve video, audio, and/or digital recording that provides the basis for analyses some time after the event has occurred. For example, Dingus, McGehee, Manakkal, Jahns, Carney and Hankey (1997) adopted a combination of digital and video recording devices during a field evaluation of a collision-warning device for motor vehicles. The aim of this design was to acquire accurate data concerning the behaviour of drivers in the operational environment. The digital data included speed and horizontal distance from the car ahead, while one of the video cameras was used to record the eye movements of participants. The other camera recorded a forward-facing view from the vehicle.

Consistent with other field evaluations, the results arising from Dingus et al. (1997) were less conclusive than anticipated in terms of establishing relationships between variables. This was due primarily to the variability associated with the operational environment, and it reflects one of the main disadvantages associated with field observation: The lack of direct control over the environment within which the study is conducted.

3.4.3   Case Study

Conventional social science research is dependent upon the acquisition of data from a broad sample of the population under investigation. However, in some cases, a broad sample is not available, and data must be acquired from a single source. This type of research strategy is referred to as a case study, and it is particularly prevalent in medicine and psychology where a patient may present unusual symptoms or behaviours.

In aviation, case studies relate primarily to the investigation of accidents or incidents. For example, Haber (1987) describes the predisposing factors associated with the crash of a low-flying fighter aircraft during military operations. Similarly, Helmreich (1994) examined some of the issues arising from the crash of an Avianca Boeing 707 near New York in 1990.

This type of research is generally exploratory in nature and provides the basis for additional study. As a case in point, Haber (1987) noted that 'this pilot probably either incorrectly perceived the far ridge as the higher of the two or failed to detect the nearer ridge at all because it blended in with the far one' (p. 524). This statement is an outcome of the analysis of the case study, and it raises a clear research question concerning the perceptual-motor ability of pilots during low-level operations.

Case studies rarely occur in isolation in aviation research and are usually designed to clarify the nature of the objects of study prior to a more detailed analysis. Nevertheless, they also provide an opportunity to describe relatively rare events (such as large scale aircraft accidents) in an effort to learn from the experience.

3.4.4 Task Analysis

According to Eckstrand (1964), the various stages associated with training system development are designed to capture accurately all the features necessary to perform a task successfully. This requires the application of distinct analytical strategies that can be divided into two categories, depending upon the extent to which they focus upon either the procedural or cognitive features involved in the performance of a task.

In its original form, task analysis was designed primarily as a process of segmenting tasks from a procedural perspective for the purposes of training and/or analysis. The application of this approach has been demonstrated in a number of domains including military operations (Patrick, 1991) and instructional systems design (Means, 1993). The primary emphasis in this type of task analysis was the segmentation of procedural and/or psycho-motor components, rather than the development of an understanding of the cognitive aspects associated with skilled performance.

However, from a training perspective, numerous authors including Klein and Klinger (1991) and Redding and Seamster (1994) have recognised the requirement for task analysis to include a cognitive dimension, in conjunction with the psycho-motor dimension. This has led to the development of a number of strategies to elicit both the cognitive and the behavioural components associated with a task. Collectively, these strategies are referred to as components of the broader discipline of Cognitive Task Analysis (CTA).

The utility of CTA in the aviation domain has been demonstrated effectively by a number of researchers in detailed examinations of the performance of air traffic controllers (Schlager, Means, & Roth, 1990; Harwood, Roske-Hofstrand, & Murphy, 1991; Redding, Ryder, Seamster, Purcell, & Cannon, 1991). Some analogies can be drawn between the tasks performed by air traffic controllers and those performed by other aviation personnel operating in dynamic and complex situations.

General agreement amongst researchers has now been reached that the development of effective training strategies is dependent upon a clear understanding of both the procedural and cognitive features associated with a complex task (Redding & Seamster, 1994). Consequently, CTA is designed to combine both the procedural and the cognitive aspects associated with the performance of a skill, although a universal, strategic, methodological approach has yet to be developed (Seamster, Redding, & Kaempf, 1997).

While other approaches devolve a task into task-related and psychologically-related components, CTA represents a more holistic approach, based upon the assumption that the two aspects of task performance are intrinsically related. Nevertheless, as Redding and Seamster (1994) indicate, there have been a number of distinct methodological strategies applied in CTA including protocol analysis, psychological scaling, performance modelling, cognitive modelling, neural network modelling, error analysis, and cognitive interviewing. Therefore, the lack of a clearly defined methodological process is one of the main disadvantages associated with the application of CTA.

3.4.5   Critical Incident Technique

The critical incident technique is a mechanism designed to trigger performance within a critical operating environment. The cognitive demands associated with these tasks are such that time is usually constrained, the environment is highly dynamic, and the consequences of an incorrect decision are extremely serious (Rouse & Vasulek, 1993). Typically, the stimulus is derived from the natural environment, and the analysis is conducted within the context of the cognitive demands which would normally occur in the situation (Klein, 1989). For example, Giffen and Rockwell (1984) designed a time-constrained, computer-based environment using aviation-related stimuli that included a vacuum-pump failure and a blocked static port.

The primary advantage associated with the critical incident technique is the potential to capture immediately the cognitive demands associated with critical operational environments (Flanagan, 1954). This tends to limit errors due to inaccuracies that may occur in either memory recall or attempts to isolate the constituent features within a laboratory environment. However, it does have a tendency to limit the breadth of cognitive strategies that can be investigated, due to the particular cognitive demands associated with critical tasks. For example, time-critical situations may, of necessity, require serial processing of information and the application of particular types of decision strategies (Wiggins & Henley, 1997).

While the critical incident technique is a relatively well accepted methodology within aviation, there are a number of conceptual difficulties involved in the nature of the approach that may limit its utility from an applied perspective. Where expert-novice differences are sought, the technique requires exposure to a situation that is sufficiently unfamiliar to initiate the cognitive features that differentiate expert from novice performance, but is sufficiently familiar to ensure that expert performance does not revert to that of a novice. Therefore, the definition of a 'critical incident' can be a matter of some considerable debate and, in some cases, a task itself may confound the results.

Kaempf, Wolf, Thordsen, and Klein (1992) recognised the difficulty associated with the analysis of critical incidents and suggested that 'non-routine' problems would represent a more appropriate source of empirical data. Since non-routine problems occur infrequently within the normal operating environment, it was assumed that successful problem resolution would involve the application of cognitive skills distinct from those skills that are applied during the course of normal operations. Moreover, experts would be expected to have a relatively greater level of familiarity with these problems due to their experience within the domain.

Although this type of comparative analysis provides an indication of differences that may exist between individuals at various levels, the difficulty arises in the development of strategies that may facilitate the acquisition of skills among less competent practitioners. Kaempf et al. (1992) attempted to overcome this problem through an analysis of non-routine events that emphasised the generation of 'rules' that might be used to assist in the successful performance of the task. However, from a skill acquisition perspective, experts typically find it difficult to elucidate the particular cues and associated actions which they use to perform otherwise automatic behaviours (Dreyfus & Dreyfus, 1986).

An allied complication associated with the critical incident technique involves the generation of simulated tasks that may not demand the level of personal involvement that might otherwise occur within the operating environment. The alternative approach is to either utilise prior experiences, or examine a situation as it occurs within the course of an operation. While the latter of these alternatives may appear optimal, the critical and time-constrained nature of the operational environment is often such that the information must be acquired retrospectively, irrespective of the experimental requirements. This is a relatively common approach to data acquisition, although the validity and reliability of retrospective protocols has been the subject of debate (see Sections 7.3 and 7.4). In particular, there is little doubt that the data arising from such analyses may be influenced by the limitations of human memory, and/or may involve some level of rationalisation (Cooke, 1994; Hoffman, 1987; Nisbett & Wilson, 1977).

While there are a number of difficulties associated with a retrospective strategy, in combination with other research strategies, it is likely to provide an effective foundation for the development of a knowledge base that might facilitate an understanding of operational behaviour in critical situations. These data may be used subsequently as the basis for more experimental research or for the development of training systems.

3.4.6   Epidemiology

The science of epidemiology arose as a result of the need to establish the etiology associated with communicable diseases (Fairbank, Jordan, & Schlenger, 1996). The main aim was to establish the particular risk factors involved in a disease in an attempt to determine the precise cause. A similar methodology has been used in psychiatry, and studies of drug and alcohol abuse.

In the aviation environment, Butcher and Hatcher (1988) advocate an epidemiological approach to the study of post-traumatic stress amongst the survivors of aircraft accidents. This type of strategy would require an examination of the factors that result in an increased risk, including the type and intensity of symptoms, the duration of the exposure, age, or familial background (Fairbank et al., 1996).

Epidemiogical analyses are designed to provide an estimate of the probability of involvement in a particular event given one or more events. For example, it might be argued that a person who smokes and whose family has a history of lung cancer would have an increased risk of contracting cancer than a person who has neither of these predisposing factors. While the probability is able to be generated from these data, it should be noted that this does not necessarily confirm that smoking **causes** lung cancer. It merely isolates smoking as a factor that increases the risk.

One of the main difficulties associated with epidemiological studies is the amount of data required to develop an understanding of the risk factors. This is particularly difficult following fatal aircraft accidents, since the social scientific information derived is often second-hand. Nevertheless, Li and Baker (1997) have conducted a detailed epidemiological analysis of the injury patterns associated with aircraft accidents and incidents, and the results provided some useful information pertaining to preventative measures.

Epidemiological studies in social science are consistent with the notion of risk analysis in system safety. Risk analysis is designed to facilitate decision-making and provide an estimate of the risk associated with various options that may be available. For example, the Civil Aviation Safety Authority (1995) sought to compare the relative risk of engine failure between twin engine piston-driven aircraft and single engine turbine-driven aircraft. The results were generated on the basis of accident data and the various local factors that were involved. These data subsequently formed the basis of an overall probability of failure for the two aircraft and, therefore, a relatively objective comparison could be made.

3.4.7   Meta-Analysis

In the age of information technology, it is often very difficult to remain abreast of all the research within a particular field. In fact, much of the research that is published in academic journals or monographs is never cited by other authors. This is due, in part, to the over-abundance of information and the lack of any coherent strategy through which to compare and contrast research outcomes.

One research strategy that does offer a solution to this dilemma is referred to as meta-analysis. This is a strategy whereby the research outcomes associated with a number of studies are combined to provide a coherent summary of the particular domain of interest. However, it should be noted that meta-analysis is distinct from a position paper, since it normally involves a quantitative analysis of the research results.

According to Christensen (1991), there are two distinct forms of meta-analysis, the first of which is designed to combine the results of a number of studies in order to increase the probability of a statistically significant result. The second strategy is designed to provide a basis to determine the overall effect of a particular strategy or intervention. For example, it may be useful to determine the extent to which scores on a particular type of questionnaire predict pilot performance. Three studies may have been completed, each of which has established a relationship between the scores on the questionnaire and pilot performance. Consequently, a meta-analysis may be used to determine the overall relationship that might be expected, either across different domains or within a particular population.

One of the main domains within which meta-analysis has been applied in the social sciences is personality and selection. This is due both to the vast body of literature in the area, and the relative lack of success in isolating the specific factors that predict successful performance within particular environments. The meta-analysis is designed to combine the prediction rates associated with a number of studies to formulate an overall perspective of the relative success of personality and aptitude tests in predicting performance (Hunter & Schmidt, 1990; Hunter & Burke, 1994; Martinussen, 1996).

An example of the application of meta-analysis can be drawn from Martinussen's (1996) examination of the research outcomes of 50 studies involving pilot selection. The aim of the study was to determine the most effective predictors of pilot performance. In this case, the research outcomes associated with individual studies were weighted to ensure that both different sample sizes and different outcome measures were taken into account (Martinussen, 1996).

Despite this strategy, comparing outcomes across different studies can be quite difficult due to both the lack of information available, and the characteristics of the particular analyses employed. In some cases, this requires a level of correction, such that a valid comparison can be made across domains. The specific strategy is known as *validity generalisation* and it is designed to provide a quantitative indication of the extent to which a selection measure can be generalised across a number of domains (Hunter & Schmidt, 1990).

Despite the advantages afforded by large sample sizes, there are number of difficulties associated with meta-analysis, the most significant of which is the reliance upon published research reports. In some cases, pertinent information may not be included, or there may be errors or *artefact* (errors due to the process of experimentation) within the data due to the nature of the sample or methodology. This typically results in a compromise, whereby the possibly of artefact is acknowledged by the researcher as part of the analytical process (Martinussen, 1996). Consequently, the results associated with meta-analyses may not necessarily yield conclusive results.

3.4.8   Survey/Interview Methods and the Nature of Data

Survey and interview techniques are amongst the most prevalent research strategies utilised within the social sciences. Surveys, in particular, are a cost-effective and relatively efficient method of acquiring data from a large sample of the population. They are typically applied when information is required concerning a series of structured topics such as attitudes to various issues, or intended voting behaviour for candidates or political parties.

Surveys differ from questionnaires in as much as the latter is normally based upon a hypothesis, whereas the former is based upon a research question. Consequently, the survey can focus upon much broader issues and need not be restricted to a central theme or notion. The advantage associated with this approach is that it allows for a much wider scope for the acquisition of data, and this can be particularly useful when little is known about a particular research domain.

For example, Hunter (1995) conducted an extensive survey of the pilot population within the United States. The aim was to determine both the extent to which pilots utilised safety-related information, and the nature of pilots' perceptions about safety-related information. This study was non-experimental in nature, since it was designed as a mechanism to describe the characteristics of the pilot population.

The format of the questions comprising a survey can vary considerably depending upon the nature of the data and the level of knowledge required concerning the domain. Where a great deal of information is known about a particular domain, it may be possible to categorise responses such that there are a number of *fixed alternatives*. These types of question might be used to categorise either qualitative or quantitative information.

In the case of fixed alternatives, qualitative information is often sought in the form of either categorical or dichotomous questions. This yields what is referred to as *nominal* data and relates to information such as sex, occupation, or ethnic background where a respondent is associated with a particular category. According to Mitchell and Jolley (1992), dichotomous survey questions are a form of categorical question, and are normally phrased in terms of membership or non-membership of a particularly category such as: 'are you male?' or 'are you female?'. This yields one of two responses (male or female), and neither response is superior in quantitative terms (Mitchell & Jolley, 1992).

However, fixed alternatives also allow for the acquisition of quantitative data in the form of *ordinal, interval* or *ratio* scales. These types of data imply a hierarchy in which one response may be superior or inferior to another in terms of its quantitative value. *Ordinal data* are based upon the principle of a ranking where a person may be asked to list a range of items in term of preference. This is distinguished from *interval data* that are ordered along a scale where the differences between two sets of sequential values is equal (Bryman & Cramer, 1994; Kerlinger, 1992; Mitchell & Jolley, 1992). For example, in terms of age, the difference between 34 and 35 is equal to the difference between 65 and 66. Where a value of zero is also possible (such as temperature), the values are referred to as *ratio data*.

In the aviation environment, interval and ratio data are useful for summarising data such as the average number of hours on task, or the maximum deviation from the glideslope during a final approach. However, perceptions and attitudes amongst participants can also be quantified and, in many cases, this type of data has been considered equivalent to interval data. For example, a researcher may be interested in determining the average level of comfort experienced by passengers on a particular long-haul, trans-oceanic route. Having completed the flight, passengers are asked to rate their level of comfort on a scale such as:

Extremely	Moderately	Uncertain	Moderately	Extremely
Uncomfortable	Uncomfortable		Comfortable	Comfortable

Each of the responses has an associated numeric value such that:

Extremely	Moderately	Uncertain	Moderately	Extremely
Uncomfortable	Uncomfortable		Comfortable	Comfortable
1	2	3	4	5

The psychological difference between each of the numeric values is assumed to be equal, thereby satisfying the requirement for interval data. This is an important assumption that has provided the basis for the development of questionnaires that summarise the perceptions or attitudes of a number of participants into a single, numeric value.

The main disadvantage associated with a fixed alternative response is that it does not allow for the qualification of responses (Kerlinger, 1992). For example, the flight may have been particularly turbulent or perhaps the menu was not as expected. This level of explanation can only be acquired through *open-ended* questions, that allow for expanded responses and provide for a more detailed description of the event.

One of the major advantages associated with open-ended questions is that they provide for unexpected responses and this can be particularly useful when conducting an exploratory study. In addition, open-ended questions can also provide an indication of the extent to which the respondent understands the nature of the question and the characteristics of the domain.

Despite the quality of the data that may be afforded by open-ended questions, there are a number of difficulties that may impact upon the data. The most significant are the time taken to complete the responses and the consequent tendency amongst respondents to skip open-ended questions included in surveys (Mitchell & Jolley, 1992). As a result, open-ended questions tend to be more effective when administered within the context of an interview schedule.

According to Kerlinger (1992), the interview schedule represents far more than simply the verbal administration of a survey. The main advantages afforded by the interview include the potential flexibility of the delivery, the motivation for the participant to be as accurate as possible, the flexibility of responses, and the level of control that can be exercised during data acquisition (Monette, Sullivan, & DeJong, 1986). However, Dyer (1995) asserts that the main criticism associated with the interview method concerns the nature of the data acquired. In dealing with this criticism, there are two main issues that need to be considered: (a) Are the data an accurate reflection of what the respondent actually **said**; and (b) Are the data an accurate reflection of what the respondent actually **meant** (see Chapter 6: Section 6.11.7).

While the outcomes of interviews will always be subject to some form of criticism, it is possible to increase the accuracy of the interpretation by using strategies including follow-up interviews, triangulation and/or the application of a mixed-methods approach. Follow-up interviews provide an opportunity for participants or Subject Matter Experts (SME) to comment on the accuracy of the researcher's interpretation of the responses elicited during the interview. This type of approach has received considerable interest in recent years, particularly from the cognitive science domain where researchers are attempting to develop expert systems (Ball, Evans, & Dennis, 1994).

In contrast to the follow-up interview, the process of triangulation involves a comparison between data acquired through a series of independent measures (Cohen & Manion, 1986; Mathison, 1988). The term *triangulation* is derived from the navigational technique of using information from multiple locations to pinpoint a specific position. In the context of the social sciences, it generally involves the consideration of data obtained from an interview, against data obtained from some other method, but which is relevant to the research question (Dyer, 1995).

According to Cohen and Manion (1986), triangulation generally involves making use of both qualitative and quantitative methods of data acquisition, and is consistent with the more contemporary, mixed-methods analytical technique. Brannen (1992) suggests that the notion of a mixed-methods approach involves more than simply the application of different methodologies. It may involve multiple investigators, different data sets, distinct theories or a combination of each (See Chapter 9: Section 9.10).

As an example, a researcher may interview a series of pilots involved in specific aircraft accidents and suggest that these pilots may have been exposed to situations for which they had not been trained sufficiently. Comparative data may be acquired through a knowledge or skills test in which the performance of similarly experienced pilots is recorded in situations comparable with the accident scenarios. This strategy is an example of a mixed-methods approach utilising quantitative and qualitative data and distinctive data sets. The aim is to provide the basis for triangulation and, therefore, the confirmation of the data acquired through the interview process.

3.4.9   Correlational Study

A correlational study is a quantitative approach to research that is designed to examine the relationship between two or more data sets (Christensen, 1991). For example, Tirre and Raouf (1994) sought to determine the relationship between perceptual-motor performance and video game experience, as part of a more detailed examination of the differences between male and female pilot recruits. The results indicated that as video game experience increased, performance during a perceptual-motor test improved. Therefore, this type of analysis has the potential to provide a descriptive, quantitative index of the strength of relationships.

One of the main advantages associated with correlational studies is that they provide the basis for predictions. Consequently, this type of research is particularly prevalent in the domain of personnel selection and training in which the aim is to select those individuals who have the potential to perform successfully within the operational environment (Burke, Hobson, & Linsky, 1997). This requires an element of prediction and, consequently, involves an examination of the relationships that exist between particular personal characteristics and subsequent performance.

The main difficulty associated with correlational studies is what Christensen (1991) refers to as the *third factor* problem. This is based upon the previous notion that variables, other than those being examined, may have an impact upon the research results. For example, the Bureau of Air Safety Investigation (1991) noted a strong relationship between the frequency of fuel starvation and the type of operation being undertaken at the time. In particular, private or business operations featured prominently in the accident and incident statistics.

Although this result may be indicative of a strong relationship, there are likely to be other variables involved that may have impacted upon the results. For example, it might be argued that private pilots might have the least recent experience amongst a group of aviators and, therefore, the incidence of fuel starvation is as much about a lack of proficiency as it is about membership of one particular part of the aviation industry. A future analysis might consider the relationship between the incidence of fuel starvation and the number of hours flown in the three months prior to the incident.

Despite the temptation to assign a causal relationship to the data, it should be noted that it is not possible to assert that one variable *causes* a change in another on the basis of the correlational studies. The notion of causality can generally be applied when one variable is manipulated and its impact is recorded against another variable. This is normally a part of the experimental research strategy.

3.4.10 Summary

Non-experimental research strategies are designed to provide a structured, methodological basis to describe the features associated with a particular domain. Each different strategy has its own advantages and disadvantages and the success of a particular strategy will depend on the nature of the particular environment within which it applies. A summary of the advantages and disadvantages associated with each strategy is provided in Table 3.1.

Table 3.1   A summary of the main advantages and disadvantages associated with various types of non-experimental research strategies

	Advantages	Disadvantages
Secondary Records	Ease of Access	Lack of Control over Data
Field Observation	Naturalistic Setting	Lack of Control
	Unobtrusive Observer	Cannot Identify Causal Relationships
		Time Consuming
Case Study	Targets Unusual Cases	Cannot Identify Causal Relationships
	Notion of Realism	Lack of Generalisation
		Individual Differences
Task Analysis	Structured Approach	Time Consuming
Critical Incident Technique	Triggers Cognitive Functions	Differential Effect on Individuals
	Differentiation between Groups	Undue Stressors on Participants
Epidemiology	Objective Comparisons	Large Amounts of Data
	Integrates Data	Does not Indicate Causality
Meta-Analysis	Large Sample Sizes	Assumptions
		Lack of Control over Data
Survey	Cost Effective	Lack of Control over Data
	Large Sample Size	Limited Responses
Interview	Variety of Responses	Time Consuming
	Testing within the Domain	Small Sample Sizes
		Subject to Biases
	Control over Data	Amount of Data Acquired
Correlational Study	Descriptive Index of Relationships	Third-Factor Problem
	Facilitates Predictions	No Causality

Despite the differences between the various forms of non-experimental research strategies, they should not be considered mutually exclusive. Most researchers employ a combination of non-experimental strategies to fulfil particular research goals. For example, the use of surveys and interviews is an important part of other research strategies such as task analysis, critical incident analysis, and correlational research. Consequently, non-experimental research ought to be considered as a series of complementary strategies that are designed to facilitate the development of a coherent and accurate description of human behaviour within a particular environment.

3.5   Experimental Research

Whereas non-experimental research strategies tend to be associated with describing behaviour within a particular environment, experimental research is designed to focus upon the acquisition of universal knowledge that is generally independent of a specific domain (Kerlinger, 1992). It is typically based upon the notion that by accounting for the impact of extraneous variables, it is possible to determine the impact of the manipulation of one variable on changes that occur within another. This provides the basis for the conclusion that changes in one variable *cause* a particular effect in another. It should be noted that this type of conclusion could not be reached on the basis of correlational research.

An example of experimental research can be derived from an investigation of the impact of incentives on learning a repetitive decision task, conducted by Hogarth, Gibbs, McKenzie, and Marquis (1991). The decision task required participants to respond to a computer-generated cue by estimating an appropriate response. Two groups of participants were used during the study. The first group was told that the remuneration for the experiment would not be dependent upon performance (no incentive). The second group was told that performance accuracy would impact upon the amount of remuneration received. Consequently, participants in the latter group were expected to experience some level of incentive to complete the task successfully.

Performance during the task was calculated by subtracting the participant's estimation from the actual value and then subtracting this value from a constant of 500 (Hogarth et al. 1991). By varying the level of incentive provided to participants, it was hypothesised that this would impact upon performance during the task.

From a research perspective, the variable 'incentive' is being **manipulated** by the researcher in this case and, therefore, it is referred to as the *independent* variable. The variable 'performance' is being **measured** by the researcher and, therefore, it is referred to as the *dependent* variable. The distinction between independent and dependent variables is particularly important in experimental research designs, since the terms clearly isolate the nature of any causal relationship that is expected to emerge (see Section 3.3).

The causal nature of experimental research also requires that particular research designs be employed, the main two being after-only designs and before-after designs (Christensen, 1991). The appropriateness of a particular design will be dependent upon the hypothesis under investigation.

3.5.1   After-Only Designs

The after-only design involves the division of participants into two or more groups. Each group is subject to some form of treatment or intervention such as training, exposure to a drug, or emotional arousal (see Figure 3.2). In this case, the type of treatment or intervention that participants receive reflects a particular level of the independent variable. Participants are tested (measured) following exposure to the treatment or intervention, and comparisons are made between groups. The variable that is measured is the dependent variable.

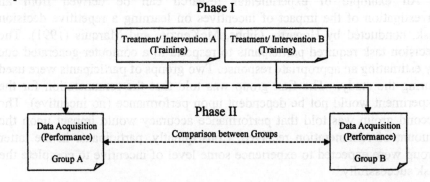

Figure 3.2   An illustrative example of the after-only design using two groups each of which receives a different treatment or intervention

After-only designs are useful for tasks such as examining the impact of a training schedule on performance. However, it should be noted that unless extraneous variables can be controlled or accounted for, the research design is quasi-experimental, rather than experimental per se.

The research conducted by Hogarth et al. (1991) is an example of an after-only research design in which two groups were provided with a different intervention (level of incentive), and performance was compared subsequently (see Section 3.5). The main advantage associated with this type of research strategy is that it provides a clear and independent comparison between the relative impact of two or more independent variables on one or more dependent variables.

Box 3.2

An example of an after-only design

In the case of our experiment involving the effects of alcohol on flying performance, an after-only design would require at least two groups of participants. The first would act as a control group, and would be tested in the absence of alcohol. However, the second group would act at an experimental group, and alcohol would be administered prior to testing. If the experiment involves different levels of alcohol, we might increase the number of experimental groups that we use.

To ensure that a valid comparison can be made between the two groups, the participants must be matched for features such as age and sex. If one group contains predominantly older participants, it may have an impact on the results, independent of the effects of alcohol.

The difficulty associated with the after-only design is that the success of the approach is dependent upon the nature of the groups. For example, when one group is compared against another group following exposure to a training program, it may be necessary to match participants prior to the intervention. This involves identifying the characteristics of participants prior to testing, and ensuring that, for every characteristic in one group, there is a balance in the other. The aim is to ensure that any individual differences that exist between the groups will have a minimal impact upon the results of the analysis.

3.5.2   Before-After Designs

Unlike the after-only design, the before-after design relies upon the acquisition and comparison of data both before and after an intervention or treatment (see Figure 3.3). This type of design is particularly useful for testing the effects of medical interventions, since the effects can be quite different for different individuals. The main advantage associated with the before-after design is that it is possible to take into account the impact of individual responses due to factors such as age, sex, or experience (Christensen, 1991). This is also referred to as a *repeated measures* strategy, and it is designed to overcome some of the problems associated with the after-only design.

The before-after experimental research design provides the researcher with the greatest level of control over the factors that impact upon subsequent performance. However, the difficulty is that there is often a need to control for variables that may occur as a part of the intervention process. A relatively well-known example in this regard is referred to as the 'placebo effect'.

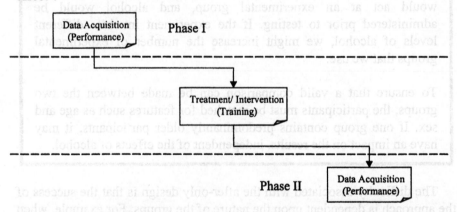

Figure 3.3   An illustration of the before-after design in which data are acquired both before and following an intervention or treatment

The placebo effect is a psychosomatic response in which a participant experiences the symptoms associated with a drug, the basis of which is psychological, rather than physiological. For example, researchers have demonstrated that participants will experience those symptoms that they are 'expected' to experience, even though a sugar pill (placebo) has been administered (Lloyd, Mayes, Manstead, Meudell, & Wagner, 1990). Consequently, the nature of some before-after designs may render it impossible to determine the extent to which a particular response was actually the product of the intervention, rather than a placebo effect.

One strategy to overcome the placebo effect is to employ a combination of the after-only and before-after designs. This type of strategy involves the use of a repeated-measures design in combination with a control group, and it provides for maximum control over extraneous variables. However, it does require a larger sample than either of the two designs in isolation.

Box 3.3

An example of a before-after design

If we were to use a before-after example to test the relationship between alcohol and flying performance, we would need only one group of participants. In this case, we test the group prior to the administration of alcohol, and again following the administration of alcohol.

Of course, the difficulty is in knowing whether the results were psychosomatic, or whether they were actually due to the effects of the alcohol. Therefore, we might use a placebo for some participants and determine whether there are any differences between those participants who received the placebo and those who received the alcohol. The performance of the placebo (control) group in the before-after design would also tell us whether there were any effects due to repeated practising of the task.

3.5.3 Summary

While there are distinct advantages associated with the application of experimental research designs (see Table 3.2), one of the main difficulties associated with this approach is the extent to which the results can be applied beyond the laboratory. Moreover, some practitioners question whether purely experimental research can be applied to solve 'real-world' problems (see Banaji & Crowder, 1989). Generally, this perception stems from the reductionistic nature of experimental research that is designed to limit or control for the impact of extraneous variables.

However, it is important to recognise that there are particular areas of research that demand an experimental approach. This type of experimental research may provide the basis for the development of solutions to applied problems. For example, chemistry is one domain in which a highly structured experimental research design has led to the development of new composite materials that have application in medicine, packaging, and production.

Table 3.2   A summary of the main advantages and disadvantages associated with two types of experimental research strategies

	Advantages	Disadvantages
After-Only Designs	Facilitates Comparisons between Independent Groups	Difficult to Control for Individual Characteristics
	Allows for the Control of Extraneous Variables	May be Difficult to Generalise to the Applied Environment
Before-After Designs	Facilitates Comparisons within Groups	May be Subject to Placebo and/or Practice Effect
	Facilitates the Control of Individual Characteristics	May be Difficult to Generalise to the Applied Environment
	Allows for the Control of Extraneous Variables	

Experimental research within social science poses some difficulties due to the complexity of human behaviour. Moreover, behaviour often occurs in response to situational cues (Hess, 1987). Consequently, there may be a need to implement both experimental and non-experimental procedures in applied settings.

3.6   Quasi-Experimental Research

As the term suggests, *quasi-experimental research* is based upon an experimental design that does not necessarily meet all of the requirements for classification as experimental research (Christensen, 1991). For example, Adelman, Cohen, Bresnick, Chinnis, and Laskey (1993) sought to determine the impact of different expert system interfaces on the cognitive performance of United States Army air defence operators. Since the participants were not part of a random selection, the study does not meet the requirements for experimental research. Nevertheless, Adelman et al. (1993) did adopt an after-only experimental design in which participants were examined having been exposed to two different interfaces.

Quasi-experimental research is generally based upon the after-only and before-after experimental designs, but may be applied within a wide variety of operational settings. The main factors that distinguish quasi-experimental research designs from experimental research designs include:

- Unequal numbers of participants in groups;
- Unequal data points;
- History effects (age, sex); and
- Interrupted time series (adapted from Christensen, 1991)

These factors tend to be characteristic of the unpredictable nature of applied research and, therefore, quasi-experimental research designs tend to be used relatively frequently in applied research (Hedrick et al. 1993). Two of the more common strategies associated with quasi-experimental research include longitudinal and cross-sectional research strategies.

3.6.1   Longitudinal Research

Longitudinal research can be either experimental or non-experimental, and is designed to investigate changes that occur within variables over time (Christensen, 1991; Mitchell & Jolley, 1992). For example, it might be argued that the ultimate test of the success or otherwise of a training strategy is the extent to which it provides the basis for successful performance within the operational environment over a long period of time. Consequently, trainees may be examined shortly after the completion of a training course, and then periodically throughout their careers. To ascertain the relative success of the training course, the performance of trainees may be compared against the performance of a control group who had not been exposed to the training.

The main advantage associated with a longitudinal research strategy is that the variables are tested over long periods of time. This may be appropriate for research areas such as Crew Resource Management (CRM), hazard identification and reduction, drug analyses, and/or post-traumatic stress for which the impact may emerge over the longer-term.

However, despite the advantages afforded by longitudinal research in terms of observing phenomena over a long period of time, there are a number of issues that may restrict the extent to which definitive conclusions can be drawn. For example, longitudinal research in the social science domain is subject to a lack of direct control over extraneous variables. Therefore, it often requires a large sample of both participants and data points to ensure that any changes that emerge can be reliably traced to their origin.

In addition to the difficulties associated with obtaining reliable data, longitudinal research is also relatively time consuming, and is subject to a delay in formulating coherent responses to research questions and hypotheses. One mechanism to overcome the latter problem involves a cross-sectional analysis.

3.6.2   Cross-Sectional Research

The cross-sectional research strategy is generally based upon the after-only experimental strategy in which two distinct groups are compared against consistent criteria. Instead of testing a cohort over a period of time (as in the longitudinal strategy), the cross-sectional strategy examines a cross-section of a sample such as experts and novices, or younger and older pilots.

Expert-novice comparisons, in particular, have adopted the cross-section research strategy as a means of both establishing the bases of expert systems and/or facilitating the development of training strategies (Wiggins & O'Hare, 1993). The main advantage associated with the cross-sectional research strategy is the relative ease with which data can be acquired. However, it is also subject to potential biases associated with the selection of possible participants. For example, novices differ from experts in many ways other than simply task-oriented experience. There may be individual differences in age, ability, social and familial background, and/or level of education. Each of these factors may impact upon the final results.

3.6.3   Summary

Although quasi-experimental research designs provide greater flexibility than that afforded by experimental designs, it should be noted that quasi-experimental designs increase the probability that the results obtained will not be explained completely by the independent variables. Consequently, a level of uncertainty is often associated with quasi-experimental research, and this tends to limit the extent to which the results can yield absolute solutions. In selecting an appropriate quasi-experimental research design, it is important to consider the nature of the research questions or hypotheses (see Table 3.3). However, this process should occur in concert with a consideration of the particular non-experimental or experimental strategy upon which the study is based.

3.7   Choosing between Research Strategies

For the novice researcher, choosing between research strategies can be a particularly daunting task. The decision tree in Figure 3.4 is designed to simplify matters. By answering the questions in sequence, it should be possible to limit the available research strategies to two or three options.

Irrespective of the type of strategy adopted, there will always be advantages and disadvantages that must be taken into account. Generally, the type of research strategy employed should be guided by the characteristics associated with the research questions or hypotheses.

Table 3.3   A summary of the main advantages and disadvantages associated with two types of quasi-experimental research strategies

	Advantages	Disadvantages
Longitudinal Research	Acquisition of Data over Long Periods	Time Consuming
	Facilitates a more Detailed Understanding of Behaviour	Large Sample Size Required to Obtain Reliable Results
		Lack of Control over the Research Setting
Cross-Sectional Research	Rapid Data Acquisition	Data may be Subject to the Environmental Setting
		Data May not Reflect 'Real-world' Relationships

3.8   Chapter Summary

This chapter was designed to introduce the various classes and strategies of research design. A distinction was made between the three classes of research: non-experimental, experimental, and quasi-experimental. The non-experimental approach is generally used in response to a research question, while the experimental approach is more appropriate for the hypothetico-deductive method. Quasi-experimental designs are similar to experimental strategies, but fail to meet all the necessary requirements for the control of extraneous variables.

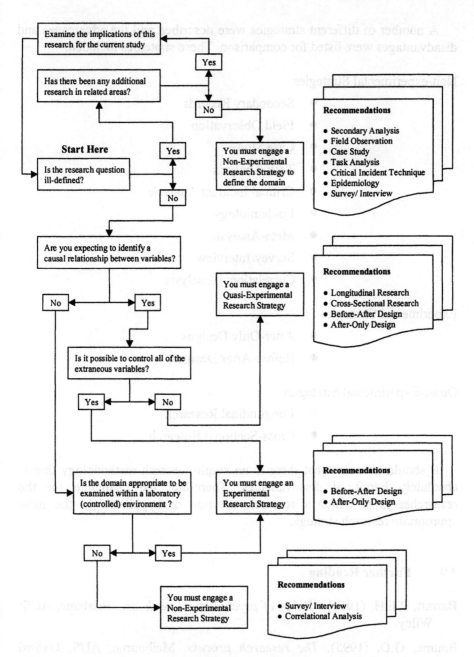

Figure 3.4 Decision tree to assist in the identification of an appropriate research strategy

A number of different strategies were described and the advantages and disadvantages were listed for comparison. These strategies included:

Non-experimental Strategies

- Secondary Records
- Field Observation
- Case Study
- Task Analysis
- Critical Incident Analysis
- Epidemiology
- Meta-Analysis
- Survey/Interview
- Correlational Analysis

Experimental Strategies

- After-Only Designs
- Before-After Designs

Quasi-Experimental Strategies

- Longitudinal Research
- Cross-Sectional Research

It should be noted that there is no single research methodology that is absolutely bereft of disadvantages. Therefore, the challenge for the researcher is to match a research question or hypothesis to the most appropriate research strategy.

3.9   Further Reading

Barratt, P.E.H. (1971). *Bases of psychological methods.* Brisbane, AUS: Wiley.

Bouma, G.D. (1995). *The research process.* Melbourne, AUS: Oxford University Press.

Christensen, L.B. (1997). *Experimental methodology* (7th ed.). Sydney, AUS: Prentice Hall.

Cohen, L., & Manion, L. (1986). *Research methods in education*. London, UK: Croom Helm.

Flanagan, J.C. (1954). The critical incident technique. *Psychological Bulletin, 51,* 327-358.

Foddy, W.H. (1994). *Constructing questions for interviews and questionnaires: Theory and practice in social research*. Cambridge, UK: Cambridge University Press.

Graziano, A.M., & Raulin, M.L. (1997). *Research methods* (3rd ed.). New York, NY: Longman.

Herhog, T. (1996). *Research methods in the social sciences*. New York, NY: Harper Collins.

Hunt, M. (1997). *How science takes stock: The story of meta-analysis*. New York, NY: Russell Sage.

Kirk, R.E. (1968). *Experimental design: Procedures for the behavioural sciences*. Belmont, CA: Brooks/Cole.

McNeil, D. (1996). *Epidemiological research methods*. New York, NY: Wiley.

Salkind, N.J. (1997). *Exploring research* (3rd ed.). Sydney, AUS: Prentice Hall.

Seamster, T.L., Redding, R.E., & Kaempf, G.L. (1997). *Applied cognitive task analysis in aviation*. Aldershot, UK: Avebury Technical.

Solso, R.L., & Johnson, H.H. (1984). *An introduction to experimental design in psychology: A case approach* (3rd ed.). New York, NY: Harper & Row.

4 Ethics and Research

4.1 Introduction

This chapter begins with an analysis of the nature of research ethics and a discussion of some of the principles that are expected to guide researchers. A number of issues are examined including the responsibilities of researchers to safeguard the welfare of participants, the notion of a 'duty of care', and the security of the data that arises from research. In conjunction with the research methodology, the consideration of ethical issues forms the basis of a research proposal.

4.2 Why Ethics?

For many inexperienced researchers, ethical considerations are often considered a painful inconvenience imposed by an institution. However, the notion of ethics in contemporary social science research is as much to protect the researcher as it is to protect the participant. Adhering to ethical principles is one way to ensure that the researcher maintains a 'duty of care' towards participants and minimises the potential liability that might arise as a result of the research process.

Essentially, research ethics involves principles that are designed to guide the research process. According to Christensen (1991), these principles can be divided into three main areas:

1. Issues relating to science and society;

2. Professional issues; and

3. Issues relating to the treatment of participants.

Despite the goal that science ought to be conducted objectively, societal influences will always have an impact upon the acquisition and/or interpretation of social science data. Even the topic of research and the nature of the research question will be subject to the cultural and personal experience of the researcher. Consequently, ethical issues may arise concerning the nature and purpose of the research within society.

One issue that demonstrates the significance of this debate concerns genetic manipulation and the advances that have occurred in cloning technology. Despite the benefits that could arise from the development of cloning technology, there is considerable debate within society as to the moral aspects associated with this scientific endeavour. In fact, the National Health and Medical Research Council (NHMRC) in Australia and the Food and Drug Administration (FDA) in the United States have strict guidelines for in-vitro fertilisation, embryo transfer, the use of foetal tissue, and epidemiological research.

4.3 The Role of Scientific Research

Although scientists have the responsibility to report information without prejudice, in some cases, the information reported may be treated with disdain or outright hostility by the general population. Indeed, this occurs, despite the best intentions of scientists to report information that may be of benefit to society.

For example, the relationship between smoking and lung and heart disease is relatively well established. However, a significant proportion of young adults continue to smoke, and appear to disregard the scientific evidence available (Glendinning, Shucksmith, & Hendry, 1994). While this behaviour may be a product of social pressures rather than a rational choice, the issue is, nevertheless, indicative of the difficult relationship that often exists between science and society.

A similar situation exists in aviation, where the impact of human factors in aviation accidents and incidents has yet to be recognised by all members of the aviation industry, despite numerous publications and safety awareness strategies (Simpson & Wiggins, 1996). Indeed, some of the proponents of human factors principles in aviation may be ignored by operators, who tend to regard the domain as primarily the province of psychologists or educationalists.

Although this type of response may be disconcerting, scientists and other observers of human behaviour have a responsibility to report information factually, and without favour or prejudice. This is encapsulated within the professional responsibility of the researcher to ensure that the information that is published is as accurate and reliable as possible. According to Christensen (1991) and Kimmel (1996), the publication of fraudulent or misleading data is regarded as the most serious offense associated with the scientific profession.

4.4   Scientific Research and the Duty of Care

Part of the professional responsibility of research scientists also extends to the treatment of participants and the notion of the 'duty of care'. From a legal perspective, a researcher is in a position in which a duty of care is owed to the participant (Pengilley & McPhee, 1994). Therefore, 'reasonable care' must be taken to ensure that any foreseeable consequences that may result in injury to a participant are avoided to the maximum extent possible (Pengilley & McPhee, 1994). This may include either psychological or physiological injury, the former being more prevalent in social science research.

Milgram (1964a), in particular, provides a useful example of a potential breach of the duty of care in a study designed to examine the impact of compliance on behaviour. Each participant in the study was asked to administer an electric shock to an unseen confederate under the guise of a learning experiment. Where the confederate erred in his/her response, a simulated electric shock was administered using a 'shock generator' and the confederate responded with a yell or scream. Moreover, the 'shock generator' was equipped with labels indicating increasing levels of voltage up to a point where the confederate eventually became silent (see Figure 4.1).

In the experimental condition, two additional confederates acted to pressure the participants towards increasing the dosage administered. In contrast, the control condition occurred in the absence of the two additional confederates. A comparison between the mean voltage levels administered across the experimental and control conditions indicated that over a period of 30 trials, the mean shock level administered during the experimental condition significantly exceeded that administered during the control condition.

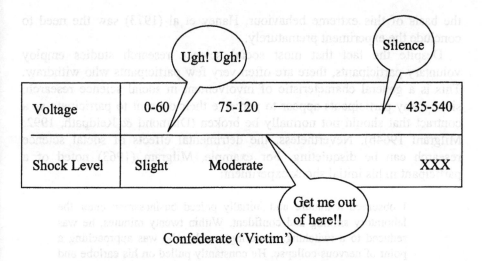

Voltage	0-60	75-120		435-540
Shock Level	Slight	Moderate		XXX

Confederate ('Victim')

Figure 4.1 An illustration of the shock levels, corresponding indications of voltage, and the responses from confederates during Milgram's (1964a) examination of compliance and human behaviour

From an ethical perspective, it should be clear that the participant was faced with a difficult dilemma: Conform to the group, or inflict a level of pain which would normally be regarded as socially unacceptable. It might be argued that this level of psychological discomfort may violate the researcher's duty of care.

The level of distress caused by some social science research can be such that studies literally have to be abandoned. A useful example of this type of situation can be drawn from Haney, Banks, and Zimbardo (1973) who sought to simulate a prison environment using undergraduate university students who were randomly assigned as either guards or prisoners. Haney et al. (1973) attempted to ensure that the simulation was as realistic as possible with prisoners being 'arrested', deloused and fitted with a prison uniform. The guards were provided with uniforms, sunglasses and a truncheon, and had absolute authority over the prisoners.

Following only five days of the simulated prison experiment, the prisoners were being prevented from going to the toilet, they were woken in the middle of the night to quote their prison numbers, and they were made to do pushups on a regular basis. Moreover, the prisoners adopted the role as prisoners and became subservient and passive in response to the guards. On the basis of this extreme behaviour, Haney et al (1973) saw the need to conclude the experiment prematurely.

Despite the fact that most social science research studies employ voluntary participants, there are often very few participants who withdraw. This is a general characteristic of involvement in social science research, since many participants appear to perceive their consent to participate as a contract that should not normally be broken (Diamond & Reidpath, 1992; Milgram 1964b). Nevertheless, the detrimental effects of social science research can be disquieting. For example, Milgram (1963) noted of a participant in his initial shock experiment:

> I observed a mature and initially poised businessman enter the laboratory smiling and confident. Within twenty minutes, he was reduced to a twitching, stuttering wreck, who was approaching a point of nervous collapse. He constantly pulled on his earlobe and twisted his hands. At one point, he pushed his fists to his forehead and muttered: "Oh God, let's stop it". And yet he continued to respond to every word of the experimenter and obeyed to the end (p.377).

While it is unlikely that research studies such as Milgram's (1963; 1964a) would be countenanced within the contemporary research environment, Milgram (1964b) himself argues that some areas of research are, by their very nature, likely to lead to difficulties for participants. However, this should not prevent the researcher from investigating these issues.

Baumrind (1964) takes issue with Milgram's (1963; 1964a) research arguing that the researcher ought to possess an interest in the welfare of participants and ensure that they are not subjected to any discomfort as a direct result of participation in research, and that adequate debriefing is provided as appropriate. Herein lies the dilemma for researchers in terms of participant welfare. Of necessity, and in the interest of participant welfare, some areas of research will automatically be excluded from investigation.

In the aviation environment, the same dilemma applies. For example, testing within the operational environment increases the exposure of the participant to the consequences of errors. As a result, a significant proportion of aviation-related research is conducted within a simulated environment, despite the consequent limitations associated with this type of research setting.

Box 4.1

Real world versus laboratory settings

One of the difficulties that we face with our study concerning the effects of alcohol on performance is the extent to which we can expect to observe behaviour as it would occur within the operational environment. Although we are seeking to determine the impact of alcohol on operational performance, it would be highly unethical, dangerous, and illegal to administer alcohol and then ask participants to operate a *real* aircraft. In this case, we have little choice but to use a simulator and extrapolate the results to the operational environment.

Partly in response to this type of ethical dilemma, a number of organisations, including the American Psychological and Anthropological Associations, have developed ethical principles as a guide for the conduct of research. The aim is to provide a basis upon which researchers can formulate decisions in the interests of both the participants and the research outcomes.

4.5 Ethical Principles

Ethical principles are designed to offer a guarantee of behaviour, particularly within organisations in which there is a dependent relationship with clients. Banks, universities, government organisations, and most professional bodies profess to operate according to ethical principles. Adherence to these principles is largely voluntary, although there can be serious consequences for a breach of ethical principles (Rosnow & Rosenthal, 1997).

Apart from the adverse publicity that arises from such a breach, there may be more punitive consequences in some cases, such as the loss of research funding, and/or exclusion from a professional organisation or association. Most importantly, a breach of ethical principles may result in a loss of confidence amongst participants, particularly in terms of their future involvement social science research.

Box 4.2

Ethical principles and alcohol

Although we may have taken into account the requirement to test participants in the relative safety of a flight simulator, there are a number of other ethical issues to consider, particularly since we are using a drug such as alcohol. For example, we will have to determine whether any potential participants have a history of alcohol problems. Clearly, those people with a history of alcohol problems should not be included as participants.

We will also have to determine the extent to which the alcohol will have an impact upon participants' behaviour after the study has been completed. A researcher cannot advocate driving or operating machinery until participants' blood-alcohol is within the legal and/or operational requirements. As a result, participants may have to be monitored until the effects of the alcohol have diminished.

Finally, we have to think about the type of data that we expect to collect. For example, if we collect data using a video or audio recording, we have to determine how we will maintain the confidentiality of the participants, how we will secure the information, and how long we will keep this information after the study. Furthermore, we have to be aware that participants have the ethical right to examine any recordings that we make, and can elect to withdraw any or all of the information from subsequent analysis.

Ethical principles guide the process of research in a number of ways including the types of participants who are selected, and the mechanisms used to secure and manage the data. In particular, researchers have a responsibility to maintain the security of the data and safeguard the anonymity of participants.

Where video or audio recordings are made, participants must give explicit consent to the use of recording devices, and they retain the right to review any recordings and withdraw the use of any information as necessary. Normally, recordings must be erased once the material has been transcribed for analysis, although the raw data should be retained for at least five years.

4.6 Ethical Principles of the APA

According to Rosnow and Rosenthal (1997), the impetus for the development of the ethical principles of the American Psychological Association (APA) was, amongst other factors, the increasing proliferation in the 1960s of so-called 'deception studies'. According to Kimmel (1996), deception studies can be classified as involving either 'active deceptions' or 'deceptions by omission'. Studies involving the former engage in strategies in which:

- There is a misrepresentation of the purpose of the research;
- The researcher's identity is withheld from participants;
- Confederates are used;
- Inaccurate promises are made;
- There is a violation of the requirement for anonymity;
- Inaccurate information is provided concerning the research procedures;
- There are inaccurate explanations of the purposes of research equipment;
- Inaccurate diagnoses are made;
- Placebos are used; and/or
- The participant is misled as to the nature of the experimental setting

Research methodologies involving deceptions by omission include:

- Observations that are concealed;
- Intentional provocation; and/or
- Secret recordings

While the APA's ethical principles do not exclude the possibility of deception studies, they do provide a series of guidelines that are designed to safeguard the welfare of participants (American Psychological Association [APA], 1992; Sommer & Sommer, 1980). In particular, where deception may be required, researchers have an ethical obligation to conduct a debriefing in which participants are advised of the true nature of the study and there is opportunity to assess any adverse reactions that may have arisen (APA, 1992; Kimmel, 1996). Moreover, the use of deception requires that researchers do not use such physical or psychological risks that would otherwise prevent individuals from participating (APA, 1992).

One of the most significant aspects of participation in research involves the notion of 'informed consent'. Under normal circumstances, the APA (1992) recommends that researchers advise potential participants of the precise nature of the research, and that they are free to withdraw from the study at any time, and without obligation. In addition, researchers are expected to explain to participants, those factors that may influence their willingness to participate including any risks of injury or discomfort, potential adverse reactions, and/or limitations concerning the confidentiality of data arising from the study (APA, 1992).

While informed consent is not necessarily required for the completion of anonymous questionnaires, it should be noted that, in this case, it is not possible to acquire information that might be used to identify participants. In the aviation environment, the number of flying hours might be acquired in addition to the participant's position within an airline. Depending upon the size of the airline, it may be possible to identify participants and, therefore, informed consent may be required in this type of situation.

Where research involves the use of subordinates or individuals with whom there is a dependent relationship, researchers must ensure that there is no recourse against participants, should they choose to withdraw from the study (APA, 1992; Kimmel, 1996). Moreover, researchers ought to take care when offering excessive inducements for participation. This is not only regarded as unethical, but it may also impact upon the methodological aspects of the study, since the sample is no longer random.

In summary, the main principles of research ethics advocated by the APA (1992) include:

- The provision of informed consent (where appropriate);
- Minimising the invasiveness of the data acquisition process;

- Avoiding deception where possible (Otherwise, employ a debriefing session and minimise the exposure of participants to discomfort or adverse reactions);
- Avoiding excessive inducements for participation;
- Honouring commitments made to participants;
- Minimising the exposure to discomfort;
- Including a debriefing session; and
- Maintaining the dignity and welfare of the participant.

(Adapted from APA, 1992; Kimmel, 1996; Sommer & Sommer, 1980)

Despite the fact that these principles were developed for the purposes of psychological research, they remain appropriate for any type of social science research. Moreover, they remain applicable within any domain, including aviation.

4.7   Consent Forms and the Provision of Information

During the course of a normal research project, participants will be asked to complete a consent form indicating that they understand the nature of the study and that they have the option of withdrawal at any time. A fundamental aspect of the notion of informed consent is an accurate understanding of the nature of the research project.

Although this process may be accomplished through a verbal briefing, the optimal strategy involves the administration of an information sheet (see Box 4.3), some time prior to the completion of the consent form. This ensures that participants have sufficient time to consider the nature of the research project and their willingness to participate.

The administration of a consent form (see Box 4.4) provides a contractual arrangement between the researcher and participants, and it is a mechanism to protect the researcher against subsequent litigation. The administration of both information sheets and consent forms are relatively common strategies to fulfil the ethical requirement for informed consent. However, researchers should explain, in as much detail as possible, any other ethical issues that may impact upon the wellbeing of the participants engaged in the research study.

4.8   Ethics Committees

Most institutions in which research is conducted will have committees that consider the ethical and methodological aspects of research proposals. These committees typically include a combination of researchers, lawyers, lay-persons and other interested parties to ensure that the committee's perspective is as representative as possible of both the needs of researchers, and the perceptions of the community. It should be noted that the acquisition of data cannot commence until approval has been obtained from all of the relevant authorities.

One of the main roles of ethics committees is to balance the anticipated outcomes of the research against the needs of participants. Where a researcher has not established the anticipated outcomes, the ethics committee may reject a proposal as unlikely to yield information sufficient to warrant the investment of time and resources. Therefore, it is important that researchers consider aspects such as the value of the research and the likelihood that the research will yield productive and useful outcomes.

Part of this process involves the development of a clear and coherent research question and an appropriate methodology. In some cases, ethics committees will also seek information concerning the data analytical techniques that will be used. Consequently, it is important that researchers establish a research proposal in which these questions can be considered and addressed subsequently.

4.9   Chapter Summary

This chapter considered the ethical principles associated with research in general, and research within aviation in particular. These principles were discussed in terms of the relationship between science and society, professional issues, and the care, privacy and dignity of participants. It was emphasised that the ethical basis of research is a part of aviation inquiry that should not be underestimated.

Box 4.3

An example of an information sheet

Information Sheet

Alcohol Effects and Pilot Performance

This study is designed to determine the impact of alcohol on pilot performance. You will be asked to complete three trials, each of which will involve the ingestion of a different amount of alcohol. These trials should take no more than 30 minutes, and you are free to withdraw at any time during the study.

The trials will be completed in a full-motion flight simulator, and will involve a series of standard manoeuvres, each of which is designed to examine your ability to operate an aircraft within certain limits. You will be monitored at all times throughout the study, and any adverse reactions arising from the ingestion of the alcohol will result in the immediate termination of the study.

Please note that you are under no obligation to complete this study and you may withdraw at any time. In addition, the results of this study will remain secure and confidential, and will not have any bearing on your employment within this airline.

We appreciate your participation in this study and if you have any questions, please do not hesitate to contact _____ on:

Telephone
Fax

Box 4.4

An example of a consent form

Consent Form

Alcohol Effects and Pilot Performance

I have been asked to participate in the research _____ conducted by _____, and give my free consent by signing this form. I understand that:

The research project will be carried out as described in the Information Sheet, a copy of which I have retained. I have read and understood the Information Sheet and have had the opportunity to have all my questions answered to my satisfaction; and that

My consent to participate is voluntary and I may withdraw from the study at any time. I do not have to give a reason for the withdrawal of my consent.

Signature .... Date / / 9

I wish to receive a summary of the overall results of this research. Please send a summary to me at the address below on completion of the study.

Name: _____

Address:_____

4.10　Further Reading

American Psychological Association. (1982). *Ethical principles in the conduct of research with human participants.* Washington, DC: Author.

Australian Psychological Society. (1997). *Code of ethics.* Victoria: AUS: Author.

Christensen, L.B. (1991). *Experimental methodology* (5th ed.). Boston, MA: Allyn & Bacon.

Kimmel, A.J. (1996). *Ethical issues in behavioural research.* Cambridge, MA: Blackwell.

McGuigan, F.J. (1997). *Experimental psychology: Methods of research* (7th ed.). New Jersey, NJ: Prentice Hall.

National Health and Medical Research Council (1992). *Statement on human experimentation and supplementary notes.* Canberra, AUS: Australian Government Publishing Service.

Rosnow, R.L., & Rosenthal, R. (1997). *People studying people: Artifacts and ethics in behavioural research.* New York, NY: W.H. Freeman.

Solso, R.L., & Johnson, H.H. (1984). *An introduction to experimental design in psychology: A case approach* (3rd ed.). New York, NY: Harper & Row.

5 Writing a Research Proposal

5.1 Introduction

A research proposal fulfils a number of purposes, including an opportunity to consider the ethical implications associated with a research strategy. However, it is also useful as a means of establishing support from participating organisations, and/or for applying for research funding. From a researcher's perspective, the research proposal represents an opportunity to consider precisely the nature of the research question, and the type of methodology that is expected to be employed.

Typically, a research proposal will include an introductory section, a summary of the proposed methodology, a consideration of data management and analysis, budgetary requirements, and a summary of any anticipated benefits of the research. The aim is to provide as clear a picture as possible of the nature and objectives of the research. Where necessary, it may also be necessary to include ethical considerations such as the security of data.

5.2 Research Proposal: The Introduction

In many ways, the introductory section of a research proposal will be similar to the introductory section that is included in a final research report or publication. However, it should be noted that the proposal is generally written for a wider audience than the final report. Moreover, the readership of the research proposal will not necessarily be aware of the technical jargon or research terminology that is used within the particular field of research (Leach, 1991). Consequently, technical and research terminology may need to be explained in greater detail than would normally be the case in a technical publication.

The normal course of an introductory section would be expected to include a brief description of the research problem followed by a critical examination of the prior research within the area. Within the social sciences, prior research is typically discussed from either a 'theme-based' perspective or a 'historical' perspective, depending upon the characteristics of the domain and the nature of the research problem. For example, in the field of decision-making, there have been a number of different strategies that have been proposed over the years. These strategies can generally be classified as either prescriptive or descriptive accounts (Garriba, 1986). Therefore, an introduction to this area of research might involve a critical comparison between the relative merits of each type of account in terms of facilitating decision-making performance. In this way, a theme-based approach would have been developed in preference to a historical approach.

Where an author seeks to convey a particular sequence of changes or events, a more historical approach may be appropriate. For example, Koonce (1984) presents an historical account of the history of aviation psychology in which the sequence of events is the issue that is most important in terms of establishing the relevance of the information discussed.

Irrespective of the particular approach undertaken during the introductory section, there is a requirement to ensure that the argument progresses towards clear and concise research questions and/or hypotheses. Moreover, these research questions and/or hypotheses should represent a logical culmination of the previous discussion, and should include some reference to the current state of knowledge. Having read the introductory section to the research proposal, the reader should be aware of:

1. The nature of the research question;
2. The relevance of the research question;
3. How and why the research question has been examined previously;
4. The current knowledge about the area;
5. The expected outcomes and the anticipated achievements;
6. How the question will be answered; and
7. The form that the data analysis will take.

5.3   Methodology

Consistent with the final report, the methodological section of a research proposal should include a consideration of the potential participants, a description of the proposed apparatus or materials to be used, an explanation of the research design where appropriate, and a summary of the proposed procedure.

5.3.1   Participants

When considering the proposed participants, it is important to establish the specific characteristics of the sample that are required for the study. In particular, demographic factors such age, sex and experience need to be taken into consideration in terms of their impact upon the experimental methodology. Older participants may react differently to specific tasks than younger participants performing the same tasks. Where this is likely to be a factor, either the sample needs to include a balance of younger and older participants, or one group may need to be excluded during the recruitment phase. However, it is important to note that the latter approach will restrict the extent to which the results may be generalised across a range of age groups.

Within the aviation environment, one of the most pervasive constraints to participation in the research process involves the perception of the confidentiality of the data. Operational personnel, in particular, can be extremely suspicious of performance-based appraisals, and will require an assurance that the information will be de-identified and will remain confidential. Maintaining a level of confidentiality can be difficult where small sample sizes are employed. Therefore, it is necessary to explain clearly how confidentiality will be assured, and the extent to which employers or regulatory authorities will have access to the raw data.

5.3.2   Apparatus and Materials

The apparatus or materials section of the research proposal needs to include a clear description of the physical resources that will be required to conduct the research. Where equipment is required, the type of equipment and the strategies necessary to obtain access to this equipment need to be specified. In the case of materials such as questionnaires or surveys, these need to be described in detail and included in an appendix. This ensures that the reader is fully aware of the nature of the data being sought during the research process.

5.3.3   Experimental Design

In the case of quasi-experimental and experimental research (see Chapter 3), a factorial design may be employed where comparisons are made between or within groups. This information should be specified within the design section of the proposed methodology, as it provides a concise summary of the independent and dependent variables that are involved in the study.

The purpose of a factorial design is to determine the effect of one or more 'factors' (or independent variables) on one or more dependent variables. For example, Beringer and Harris (1997) sought to determine the impact of four automation-related malfunctions on a series of indicators of pilot performance including the position of the aircraft, and the state of critical switches (such as the autopilot disconnect) at various times throughout the scenario. In this case, a single factor was involved (automation-related malfunction) for which there were four levels (command-over roll, soft roll, soft pitch, and runway pitch trim-up). According to Beringer and Harris (1997), these four characteristics are regarded as common aircraft responses following an autopilot failure.

Given that there was a single factor manipulated in the study, and that participants were to be exposed to all four levels of the factors (within-subjects or repeated-measures), the study can be summarised in the design section as:

a single-factor (automation-related malfunction), within-subjects design, incorporating four levels (command-over roll, soft roll, soft pitch, and runway pitch trim-up).

Box 5.1

Experimental design

We are now faced with some important decisions concerning our study of the relationship between alcohol and pilot performance. Guided by previous research and theory, we might specify three levels of the alcohol variable (none, low, and moderate) and three levels of age of particpants (25-34; 35-44; 45-54 years). This gives us what is referred to as a two-factor or two-way, 3 x 3 design (see below). Notice that, in this case, we have specified that different participants be used in each of the nine conditions. An alternative to this approach will be discussed at a later stage.

Factor Two (Age)

		25-34 Years	35-44 Years	45-54 Years
Factor One (Alcohol)	Moderate	No. of Participants	No. of Participants	No. of Participants
	Low	No. of Participants	No. of Participants	No. of Participants
	None	No. of Participants	No. of Participants	No. of Participants

Three Levels

Three Levels

If we use 20 participants in each of the conditions, we will need to run 20 x 9 = 180 separate experimental sessions. If it takes an hour to complete the experiment, you can see that this relatively simple design could be quite labour-intensive. For this reason, it is suggested that the number of independent variables and their levels be kept to a minimum. Notice that if we simply add one more two-level variable to our design, such as the time of test (day or night), then it would blow out to an 18-cell design requiring 360 experimental sessions (testing hours)!

Describing the experimental design in this manner is useful for a number of reasons. It alerts the researcher to the size and scope of the experiment in terms of the required number of participants and testing hours. In addition, drawing the variables and their levels in box form is an effective method for explaining the design when the study and results are to be presented. More importantly, the experimental design provides an indication of the kind of statistical analysis that will later be required to analyse the data.

5.3.4 *Procedure*

The procedure section of the proposal is normally described in as much detail as possible, and from the perspective of the participant. The aim is to describe precisely the interaction that is expected to occur between the participant and the researcher. This includes any statements or assurances that are expected to be made, and the duration of the study.

5.4 Data Analysis

A detailed consideration of the data analytical procedures is an essential part of the research proposal. In particular, it ensures that the data collected can be examined at a level that is appropriate for the particular research question or hypothesis.

For example, where qualitative data are sought, it is important to ensure that the information acquired is sufficiently broad to enable detailed conclusions to be drawn (Miles & Huberman, 1994). In some cases, participants will raise issues that, in retrospect, would have been useful to have been included as part of the overall process of data acquisition. The consequence may be a re-examination of previous participants at a possible additional cost to the researcher and perhaps the participant.

A consideration of the data analytic process may also raise the question of the process through which qualitative data is acquired. For example, a written response may not detect the subtle nuances that might be available through audio and/or video recordings (Miles & Huberman, 1994). In addition, video and audio recordings have the benefit of establishing a context for the response (including time and date), and they also enable the data acquisition process to be accomplished retrospectively, and with minimal intervention on the part of the researcher. Finally, criteria need to be set to establish the validity and/or reliability of the data acquired (see Section 7.3 and 7.4).

Working towards quantitative outcomes, it is important to establish that all the necessary data are acquired, and that they are acquired in a format consistent with that required for the research question or hypothesis. For example, where a linear relationship is posited, the data acquired must be in either an interval or ratio format. In contrast, where a factorial design is proposed, the independent variable (factor) must be categorical, while the dependent variable must be in the form of either interval or ratio data (see Chapter 3: Section 3.4.8).

The most common error in quantitative data analysis is the failure to consider the impact of confounding factors. To eliminate the impact of these factors, it is necessary to isolate potential confounding factors at the outset either through careful experimental design or through the acquisition of additional data. These data need to be acquired during the normal process of data acquisition, such that their relative impact can subsequently be established during data analysis (see Section 3.3.1).

5.5   Budgetary Requirements

From an operational perspective, one of the most important considerations during the research process is the cost to both the operator and the research organisation. Even in cases where funding is received from outside sources, a detailed budget is a necessary requirement. A typical research budget will include anticipated expenses for at least some of the following:

- Travel (researcher);
- Travel (participants);
- The development of materials (printing and postage);
- The delivery of materials;
- Access to equipment;
- Software;
- Personnel;
- Consumables;
- Data entry and analysis;

- The purchase or lease of equipment; and/or
- Research assistance.

In addition, it may be necessary to include an estimation of the anticipated direct and indirect costs to the operator. This may include the time for participants to be interviewed, or the costs associated with the use of an operator's facilities. However, these costs should normally be allied to the anticipated outcomes of the research to facilitate a cost-benefit analysis.

5.6 Anticipated Outcomes

From both an operational and an ethical perspective, the anticipated outcomes are an essential aspect of the research proposal. The aim is to argue for the benefit of the research in terms of the information that is likely to be derived.

In some cases, the anticipated outcomes might be quite general such as 'More information will be gained concerning accident causation in the multi-crew aviation environment'. In other cases, the anticipated outcomes may be quite specific such as 'A linear relationship is expected to be established between perceptions of risk and willingness to violate aviation regulations'.

From the perspective of the operator, it is important, at this stage, to establish the gains that are expected to accrue from the research. This may be an increase in safety and/or efficiency, or it may simply be an increase in the knowledge concerning the nature of a particular problem. In either case, it will be necessary to indicate clearly the particular benefits that are likely to arise from the research, both in the short-term and in the long-term.

Generally, operationally-based organisations, such as airlines and regulatory authorities, will be seeking applied outcomes that have a measurable impact upon operational performance. For example, if funding is sought to test a new strategy to handle baggage, a specific estimate of the anticipated gains in efficiency and/or error management needs to be incorporated into the proposal. Furthermore, a cost-benefit assessment of the various alternatives might be used to further strengthen the argument and provide a justification for the investment.

5.7   Timetable

The timetable provides a clear guide for the research process and the stages at which various tasks will be accomplished. It also provides a basis against which to assess the progress of the research once it has begun. The format for timetables will differ considerably, depending upon the nature of the research and the environment within which it is being conducted. An important requirement is to ensure that all the relevant tasks are included in the timetable, and that the duration for the completion of tasks is as realistic as possible.

5.8   References

References to books, chapters, reports, and journal articles cited in the proposal should normally be included at the end of the research proposal, and they should be formatted in an appropriate style for the discipline. They represent an important part of any research paper, since they provide both a justification for the decisions made during the research process, and a basis for the reader to acquire additional information if required.

5.9   Chapter Summary

This chapter outlined the purpose and structure of a research proposal. According to McGuigan (1997), the main components of the research proposal include:

- A label for the experiment;
- A summary of previous research;
- A statement of the problem;
- A statement of the hypothesis or research question if necessary;
- A definition of the variables;
- A statement that identifies the extraneous variables and explains the way in which they will be controlled;
- An indication of the type of design to be employed;
- An indication of the process of participant recruitment and selection;

- A consideration of the ethical implications of the research;
- An indication of the types of data analyses to be used;
- An indication of the possible outcomes of the research;
- A timetable;
- Budgetary requirements; and
- An indication of the extent to which the results may be generalised.

It was emphasised that the research proposal is a significant part of the research process, since it enables the research demands to be considered and the appropriateness of the methodology to be established prior to a significant investment of resources. It also provides a very useful mechanism to clearly establish both the purpose and the anticipated outcomes of the research as might be required for justification within commercial organisations.

5.10   Further Reading

Evans, D. (1996). *How to write a better thesis or report.* Melbourne, AUS: Melbourne University Press.

Guba, E.G. (1963). Guides for the writing of proposals. In J.A. Gulbertson & S.P. Hendley (Eds.), *Educational research: New perspectives* (pp. 289-305). Danville, IL: The Interstate Printers & Publishers Co.

Locke, L.F., Spirduso, W.W., & Silverman, S.J. (1993). *Proposals that work: A guide for planning dissertations and grant proposals.* London, UK: Sage.

McGuigan, F.J. (1997). *Experimental psychology: Methods of research* (7th ed.). New Jersey, NJ: Prentice Hall.

6 Conducting Social Science Research in Aviation

6.1 Introduction

Although there are particular attractions to working within a dynamic and uncertain environment such as aviation, it is precisely these qualities that make this kind of research a relatively difficult prospect. Consequently, aviation research requires a great deal of time and commitment to ensure that the data acquired are the most accurate and reliable under the circumstances.

Chapter 6 focuses on some of the strategies and issues involved in the conduct of applied social science research in aviation. This includes a consideration of sampling technique, the development of an appropriate experimental setting, and the acquisition of sufficient support from aviation-based organisations.

In addition, there is an emphasis on the more practical aspects of the research experience, and some of the problems that can arise during the process. In many cases, these problems can be overcome through planning, and the efficient management of resources. The latter, in particular, is an essential part of research, and may include the management of research personnel and/or the purchase and maintenance of specialist equipment. Consequently, this chapter also considers the management and development of research plans and accounts.

6.2 The Process of Research

According to D.D. Woods (1988), aviation is one of a number of industrial domains that can be characterised as complex, dynamic, uncertain, and where the consequences of errors can be extremely serious. Therefore, the aviation environment offers an opportunity to examine various aspects of human performance that might not be evident in other areas. For example, aviation is one of very few domains in which operators are required to monitor equipment for lengthy periods of time, cross numerous timezones, and then perform at maximum efficiency and precision at the end of a shift.

More broadly, the aviation industry is a significant part of the world economy, and there are significant implications associated with system failures, particularly in terms of the direct and indirect costs involved. Therefore, the prevention of such failures is an attractive endeavour for researchers seeking to improve the relationship between human performance and technology. Furthermore, the results associated with this research can be applied to other areas such as the nuclear and maritime industries.

Despite the obvious attraction of the aviation industry as a research environment, there are a number of problems that may not necessarily be evident within other areas. For example, it is very difficult to simulate precisely the environmental effects that may be encountered during flight. Even in response to high-fidelity simulations, participants will report that, 'it wasn't the same' or 'I always knew in the back of my mind that it was just a simulation'. Consequently, it is very difficult to determine the extent to which the human behaviour observed within a simulated environment, is consistent with that which would occur within the operational environment.

This is a significant issue where the evaluation of training initiatives is concerned, since part of this process involves establishing the extent to which the skills developed during training have been transferred to the operational environment. Crew Resource Management training is a case in point where the transfer of training has been difficult to establish within the operational environment.

Crew Resource Management (CRM) training programs were developed throughout the 1980's and early 1990's largely in response to aircraft accidents and incidents in which a breakdown in crew coordination was cited as a causal factor (National Transportation Safety Board, 1979). However, as these training courses developed, there was a considerable level of interest in establishing the extent to which involvement in CRM courses had improved crew behaviour (Helmreich, 1984; 1987; Gregorich, Helmreich, & Wilhelm, 1990). In particular, the outcomes of this research could be used to validate the training investment on the part of airline companies, and/or ensure that the training strategies were indeed improving crew coordination.

The difficulty faced by researchers was the requirement to obtain accurate and reliable data, while maintaining an ethical approach to the research process. Covert observation of performance was excluded, since it violated ethical principles. On the other hand, more overt data acquisition strategies were equally problematic, since they may have resulted in inaccurate or unreliable responses due to the presence of an observer. This is referred to as the *audience effect* and it can have an impact upon participant performance, particularly in terms of the Hawthorne effect (see Section 6.11).

In response to this type of dilemma, Helmreich (1987) argued that it may not be necessary to evaluate crew performance, since attitudes are generally a reflection of behaviour, and the former can be evaluated through the administration of a questionnaire. Although there is some debate concerning the relationship between attitudes and behaviour (Ostrom, Skowronski, & Nowak, 1994), Helmreich (1987) has approached the problem from a slightly different theoretical perspective, and thereby avoided some of the problems associated with data acquisition within the operational environment.

Clearly, the disadvantage associated with this approach is that it is dependent upon the validity of an untested assumption. Consequently, despite anecdotal evidence to support the efficacy of CRM programs (National Transportation Safety Board, 1990a; 1990b), empirical research concerning the behaviour of crew members has generally been limited to inferences made on the basis of attitude questionnaires (Gregorich et al. 1990; Helmreich & Wilhelm, 1991; Merritt & Helmreich, 1996; Sherman & Helmreich, 1993).

6.3   The Aviation System and Research

One of the most significant characteristics associated with the aviation environment is its unpredictability. Although this is often perceived as problematic from a research perspective, it can also provide an opportunity for the acquisition of data that might not otherwise have been obtained. Nevertheless, it often results in researchers spending a great deal of time 'waiting around'.

The complexity of the aviation industry can be disconcerting to many researchers, since the development of solutions to one problem may raise issues within another aspect of the aviation environment. This is indicative of any complex system where one component is coupled with another series of components. However, the recognition of aviation as a series of interrelated components is a useful philosophical perspective that needs to be considered as an important part of the research process.

The perception of aviation as a series of interrelated components has given rise to what is referred to as the 'systemic perspective', in which changes within one aspect of the system are presumed to impact upon other aspects of the system (Maurino, Reason, Johnston, & Lee, 1995; Reason, 1990). According to Maurino et al. (1995), system failures such as accidents or incidents are, in part, a product of high-level decisions that create an environment within which safeguards and barriers against failures may be breached. Therefore, like other decision-makers within the aviation environment, researchers need to be aware of the implications on the system of both the data acquisition process and the impact of the results that emerge.

For many participants in the research process, the experience may be uncomfortable and a distraction from the main task at hand. Moreover, the audience effect may lead to failures that would not otherwise have occurred. Consequently, the decision by an organisation to conduct or facilitate research may have negative consequences in the long-term, that may not necessarily be evident at the outset.

The role of the researcher in this type of situation is to remain vigilant for those situations in which the research process is impacting upon the primary task of the operator, and withdraw as appropriate. In addition, there is a responsibility on the part of the researcher to ensure that organisations and participants are fully aware of the ethical and operational implications of the research.

6.4   Hurry Up and Wait

One of the potential negative consequences associated with the decision to conduct or facilitate research is the time limit imposed on the acquisition of data. In many cases, the uncertainty associated with the operational environment is such that compromises are made in order to acquire sufficient data within the time available. For example, testing pilots under visual flight conditions requires that the meteorological conditions be suitable for flight under Visual Flight Rules (VFR), while observing the interaction between flight attendants and aggressive passengers is dependent upon the presence of passengers who are behaving aggressively.

Where time is a limiting factor, both researchers and operators alike may be forced into situations that may not necessarily be optimal. This is characteristic of one of the most significant dangers associated with data acquisition within the operational environment, and it behoves the researcher to make it explicit to operators that safety is paramount and that data acquisition is of secondary concern. Moreover, researchers must be prepared to 'hurry up and wait' and ensure that this eventuality is factored into the research plan.

6.5   Industry Support

The nature of the aviation industry is such that most applied research initiatives will be dependent upon the goodwill of practitioners, and the support of the industry to fulfil the research goals. This support can be difficult to obtain, either for bureaucratic reasons, or for fear that the results may be detrimental to the industry.

The main issue in dealing with aviation bureaucracy is to ensure that the aims and objectives of the research are clearly explained and the benefits that can accrue from participation are identified. In many cases, researchers must be prepared to wait for official approval and this may take some time. Moreover, researchers must be prepared for a rejection, and develop a contingency plan to cope with this type of situation.

Where a particular group of individuals is targeted for research, it is essential that written permission be sought from representative organisations. For example, in the case of aircraft engineers, it may be necessary to seek permission from both participating companies and the relevant union authorities to ensure that potential participants have an opportunity to establish the implications of the research, and set guidelines as appropriate.

Establishing which is the most appropriate organisation to contact can be difficult. There are numerous organisations within the aviation industry that purport to represent various groups of aviation personnel. A list of some of these organisations, and the aviation personnel whom they represent, is listed below:

General Aviation Pilots	• Aircraft Owners and Pilots Association (AOPA)
	• Experimental Aircraft Association (EAA)
	• Flying Clubs
	• Flight Training Organisations
Licenced Aircraft Maintenance Engineers (LAME)	• Airlines
	• Maintenance Facilities
	• Union Authorities
Airline/ Commercial Pilots	• Airlines
	• Union Authorities
Flight Attendants	• Airlines
	• Union Authorities
Ultralight Pilots	• Ultralight Federation
	• Experimental Aircraft Association (EAA)
Glider Pilots	• Gliding Association
Hang-Glider/ Paraglider Pilots	• Ultralight Federation
Air Traffic Controllers	• Regulatory Authority
	• Union Authorities
Military Personnel	• Flight Safety Section

Most aviation organisations are especially apprehensive about the adverse publicity that may arise from safety-related issues. Consequently, researchers have a responsibility to ensure that, prior to publication, the results derived from the research are previewed by the organisations from whom permission was sought initially. This provides participating organisations with an opportunity to exercise a veto on all or part of the report, until an appropriate response can be developed.

One of the most important aspects of industry support is to obtain credibility for the research process in the form of an endorsement of the project by a senior official or manager within an organisation. This strategy is particularly effective in establishing the credibility of safety-related initiatives (Stone & Young, 1997), and a letter of endorsement can be attached to the information sheet as an added incentive to participate in the research initiative.

Although the aviation industry generally expresses support for research initiatives, the extent to which financial assistance can be obtained is less certain. In fact, it is unlikely that researchers external to an organisation will be offered direct financial assistance for research. More common is the provision of support 'in kind'. This might include permission to acquire data within the operational environment, the delivery of research materials (such as questionnaires) using an internal document distribution network, access to internal data or resources, the provision of transport, and/or access to the names and contact details of potential participants. Each of these strategies has an indirect cost for the organisation and, therefore, researchers need to ensure that these resources are used as efficiently as possible.

6.6   Recruitment of Participants

Part of the support offered by aviation-based organisations may involve the recruitment of potential participants. This might constitute access to contact details, and/or the distribution of an advertisement either directly, or through a publication. However, in many cases, access to contact details may be limited by privacy provisions and alternative means of acquiring participants may need to be explored.

One of the most effective means of recruiting participants is to describe the nature of the research at a meeting of potential participants. This provides an opportunity for participants to ask questions concerning the research within the relative anonymity of a group. However, it should be noted that the success of this strategy is dependent upon the capability of the researcher or speaker to provide a clear and concise summary of the research at a level that is appropriate for the audience. In addition, it is important to establish the potential gains of the research, and the outcomes for individual participants.

One of the most common methods to attract participants is to offer an incentive, either financial or otherwise. While ethical principles preclude the application of excessive inducements, it is possible to create sufficient incentive with relatively minimal levels of remuneration. An example of the impact of relatively small incentives can be drawn from Muir, Bottomley, and Marrison (1996), who sought to simulate the type of competitive environment that exists during emergency evacuations of aircraft. As an added incentive for participants, the first 50 percent of evacuees in each trial were awarded an additional £5.00 to their normal participation rate of £10.00. This resulted in extreme levels of competitive behaviour and, in some cases, trials had to be abandoned (Muir, 1994; Muir et al., 1996).

When attempting to recruit participants, researchers should note that aviation personnel are among the most tested and evaluated of all occupational groups. Moreover, there is a tendency amongst aviation personnel to be somewhat skeptical of the nature and purpose of social science research. Individuals may be reticent to participate unless there are clear, achievable goals for the research, and guarantees are made concerning the confidentiality of the data.

6.7   Data Acquisition

The acquisition of data in the operational environment can be problematic due to the diversity of locations and the lack of control over testing environments. Researchers may have to acquire data in relatively short periods of time, and with frequent interruptions. This has both methodological and practical implications for the research process, since time constraints and interruptions may impact upon the quality and the amount of data obtained.

The decision to disregard data on these grounds is a matter for individual researchers, and the main requirement is to ensure that, if contaminants are present, they impact consistently across all participants. This is equivalent to matching and, thereby, controlling for the relative impact of an extraneous variable.

By their very nature, some research designs are more likely than others to be subject to data contamination. For example, longitudinal studies require repeated measures over a long period of time and, therefore, there is a potential for a loss of data due to the lack of commitment, and/or a change in the personal circumstances of participants. In this type of design, it becomes necessary to ensure that a very large sample is available to account for the rate of attrition.

Research designs that are relatively less likely to be subject to data contamination are those that are relatively non-invasive, are perceived as relevant, and can be completed quickly and with minimal effort on the part of participants. Consequently, it is important to ensure that the research design selected is the most efficient and the most effective in terms of the acquisition of data.

Where operational data are required, it may be possible to utilise a video camera and/or audio recorder to facilitate the process of data acquisition and coding. The main advantage associated with this type of data acquisition strategy is that it allows data acquisition and analysis to occur at a later and, perhaps, more appropriate, time. This minimises the probability of data acquisition errors.

Depending upon the nature of the data, the relationship between data obtained in situ and the data obtained from video recordings can be quite high. For example, Kanki and Foushee (1989) videotaped the behaviour of flightcrew during a series of simulated critical incidents in which a great deal of crew coordination and communication was required. The aim was to record both the frequency and the types of errors that occurred amongst crews. A subsequent comparison between the data obtained in situ, and that obtained from video tapes, revealed a correspondence of 81 percent. This suggests that video recording, in particular, has the capacity to maintain the rich diversity of behaviours that occur within the operational environment

One of the main difficulties associated with the use of video and audio recordings is the level of confidentiality and anonymity that can be maintained for participants. This has been the problem with the use of Quick Access Recorders (QARs), despite the fact that they represent a rich source of useful data (Phillips, 1996). Consequently, it is important that researchers exercise a degree of caution when using video or audio data sources to maintain the confidentiality of participants.

In the case of data relating to accuracy and response latency, computer monitoring devices are often the most accurate, reliable, and convenient means for presenting stimuli and acquiring data. For example, Lintern and

Garrison (1992) were able to acquire aircraft position data at 12 hertz (cycles per second) during a simulated final approach to land. This high rate of data acquisition is only possible using computer devices. However, the difficulty is that computer monitoring devices are not usually available within the operational environment. Moreover, computer monitoring devices also tend to be highly specific in terms of the type of data acquired. Consequently, there is less flexibility to acquire additional data should the opportunity arise.

6.8   Research Planning

One of the difficulties involved in conducting applied research is the intermittent nature of the process of data collection. Therefore, it may be necessary to consider the development of a research plan as the means for structuring the collection and analysis of data. Kruithof and Ryall (1994) suggest that the development of a detailed, coherent plan is an essential prerequisite for the achievement of long-term objectives such as those involved in applied research.

The development of a research plan is normally a two-stage process, the first of which involves the identification of the tasks that need to be completed. Having isolated the various tasks, a timeline is constructed that details both the task and the duration within which the task is expected to be completed (see Figure 6.1). The tasks involved can be relatively broad, or highly specific, depending upon both the needs of the research and the characteristics of the research program.

While it is often relatively easy to develop these plans, it can be comparatively more difficult to keep to them. Consequently, it is important to maintain a level of flexibility in research planning, and include contingency strategies where necessary. Flexibility in research planning requires that when one task is awaiting completion, other tasks may progress. For example, while awaiting permission to collect data within one organisation, it may be possible to begin, or continue acquiring data within another. Similarly, the literature review and/or methodology sections may be written while awaiting clearance from an ethics committee.

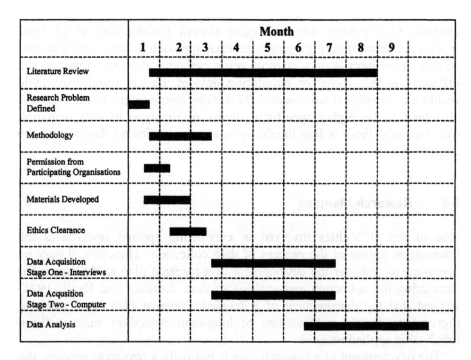

**Figure 6.1 A sample research plan illustrating the various tasks and
their duration. Note that some tasks may be undertaken in
parallel, while others are sequential**

By having more than one source for the acquisition of data, the
researcher is not only afforded a level of flexibility during the research
process, but it also provides a contingency measure if, and when, required.
Research tasks often require more time to complete than anticipated during
the initial stages of planning. This is a relatively common problem in
planning generally (Bryan, 1997), but it reinforces the need to not only
develop contingency plans, but to be as realistic as possible in developing
estimates for dates of completion.

6.9   Experimental Settings

Experimental settings within the aviation environment include laboratories,
offices, simulators, aircraft cockpits, air traffic management facilities,
maintenance hangers, and aircraft cabins. While there are advantages and

disadvantages associated with each setting, the main requirement is to ensure that it provides the appropriate amount and quality of data that is necessary to address the research question or hypothesis.

The distinction between experimental settings runs parallel to the arguments between applied and basic research. For example, applied research settings such as aircraft cockpits and air traffic control facilities provide a diverse and 'realistic' experimental setting, although the researcher has relatively less control over the characteristics of the environment. Consequently, some data may be lost or unusable due to unexpected events.

In contrast, experimental settings such as laboratories afford a degree of control, but may lack the 'realism' associated with more applied settings. Consequently, the participant may not necessarily display the behaviours or skills that are applied within the operational environment. This can create some difficulties when the researcher attempts to generalise the results to the operational domain.

Clearly, the experimental setting has the potential to impact significantly upon the behaviour of participants. Although this can create difficulties from a methodological perspective, it may also reveal some important characteristics that may not otherwise have become apparent. An example of this type of situation can be drawn from Wiggins and Henley (1997) in which a quasi-experimental setting was used to examine the decision-making characteristics associated with experienced and inexperienced flight instructors. Although the results failed to distinguish between the performance of the two groups, the methodology was able to highlight the relative inconsistency that exists in the procedures applied to formulate certain types of decisions. This result has significant implications for flight instructor training and evaluation.

6.10   Resource Management

According to Hedrick, Bickman, and Rog (1993), resource management has a major impact on the type of research design employed, and the mechanisms through which data are acquired. This is particularly the case in the aviation environment in which the costs for apparatus such as simulators and computing equipment can be exceedingly high. Consequently, there is a need to balance the type of research design employed against the costs and expected outcomes.

In addition to the costs associated with research apparatus, a significant part of the expense associated with social science research is often due to the extensive labour requirements (Hedrick et al., 1993). Therefore, it is necessary to ensure that the process of data acquisition, and the form in which the data is recorded, provide for the most efficient use of research personnel. Some of the issues for consideration might include:

- The number of participants;
- The geographic location of participants;
- The number of data points required for analysis;
- The requirement to recruit specialist research personnel;
- The type of data analytic equipment required;
- Travel costs; and
- Materials (including postage).

Researchers would normally be expected to provide a budget as part of their research proposal. While the primary aim of this strategy is to ensure that there is a reasonable cost-benefit associated with the research, it should be noted that successful outcomes often require a financial investment. In some cases, the investment can be substantial, but this always needs to be balanced against the potential benefits that may accrue from the research.

If the costs associated with a particular research project outweigh the resources available, there are a number of strategies available that might minimise the costs. One of the most obvious strategies involves an application for research assistance from government or non-governmental sources. A list of potential sources of social science research funding in aviation includes:

- Regulatory Authorities
- Insurance Companies
- Airlines
- Aviation Unions
- Safety Authorities
- Maritime Authorities and
- Aviation Associations

However, it should be noted that funding for research is relatively limited, and that alternatives may be required which minimise the potential costs. This requires a level of lateral thinking to develop alternative research designs. For example, rather than use high-fidelity simulation, it may be possible to employ PC-based simulation as a means of creating an experimental environment. Similarly, it may be possible to use computer-based data acquisition techniques, rather than transcribing information by hand. In both cases, compromises have to be made, and the impact of these compromises must be evaluated.

6.11   Possible Biases in Research

In some environments, the data acquired during the research process may be contaminated by factors other than those that are directly under investigation. Where a systematic error has occurred in the data, this is referred to as 'experimental bias' and it has the potential to manifest itself in a number of experimental effects.

6.11.1 Hawthorne Effect

The 'Hawthorne effect' takes it name from a study reported by Roethlisberger and Dickson (1939) involving the Hawthorne Relay-Assembly Plant. The researchers were commissioned to investigate strategies to improve worker productivity, and the process included a series of interviews and investigations within bank wiring and mica-splitting rooms. However, the most interesting results occurred within the relay assembly section where workers were divided into experimental and control groups.

In the case of the experimental group, changes were made to the environmental conditions including lighting and the frequency of rest periods. These changes were expected to increase the productivity of the experimental group in comparison to the control group. However, Roethlisberger and Dickson (1939) noted that improvements in performance occurred in *both* the control and experimental groups, irrespective of the changes that were initiated for the experimental group. This has since become a relatively well-known experimental artefact which Jung (1971) and Gottfredson (1996) ascribe to aspects of the observation process, rather than the interventions themselves.

From an aviation perspective, the Hawthorne effect has important implications, particularly in terms of the evaluation of safety and/or training interventions. For example, even the mere contemplation of a particular safety-related initiative may create a level of awareness amongst operators that subsequently results in an improvement in performance. Therefore, in terms of evaluation, it is important to establish whether performance-related improvements were a product of a particular training initiative, or whether the Hawthorne effect was a significant factor. Normally, the extent of this effect can only be established through comparisons between experimental and control groups (Roethlisberger & Dickson, 1939).

6.11.2 Halo Effect

The 'halo effect' refers to a bias that occurs when observers attribute an overall impression of a person's performance to ratings of more specific attributes (Cooper, 1981). For example, the impression of a particular individual as a 'good pilot' may subsequently influence an observer's ratings of attributes such as decision-making, situation awareness, or resource management. Typically, the outcome of the halo effect is a relative overestimation of performance during specific tasks (Feldman, 1986).

According to Murphy, Jako, and Anhalt (1993), the halo effect is normally assumed to occur due to the observer's inability or unwillingness to discriminate between overall performance and performance on specific attributes associated with a task. From a research perspective, this has important implications, as it may result in systematic errors in the perceptions of participant performance.

Although the halo effect is difficult to identify, there are a number of mechanisms to control for its influence including observer training, statistical control, and the pooling of results or ratings from a number of observers. In addition, ratings should always be made immediately following observation to avoid the influence of contaminating factors (Lance, Lapointe, & Stewart, 1994; Murphy et al., 1993).

6.11.3 Projection

In some cases, researchers may ascribe attributes, perceptions or behaviours to participants in the absence of direct evidence. This is referred to as 'projection bias', and it may occur either consciously or unconsciously, depending upon the nature of the research domain, and the characteristics of the investigator (Godwin & Neck, 1996).

An example of unconscious projection is provided by Neck, Godwin, and Spencer (1996) involving a case study analysis of a group of fire fighters involved in an accident that has subsequently been dubbed the *South Canyon Fire Tragedy*. The disaster occurred when 14 fire fighters were killed while attempting to extinguish a forest fire in Colorado in 1994. A subsequent report into the circumstances surrounding the accident highlighted inadequate decision-making on the part of the fire fighters as one of the most significant causal factors.

Neck et al. (1996) sought to explain the actions of the fire fighters using a theoretical principle of decision-making known as 'groupthink'. According to Janis (1983), groupthink occurs when social pressure within a group results in a reduction in the efficiency, accuracy, and/or rational judgement when formulating a decision. This phenomenon is thought to have been influential in the decision to launch the space shuttle Challenger, which disintegrated shortly after launch in 1988 (Esser & Lindoerfer, 1989).

Neck et al. (1996) contend that an analysis of the South Canyon Fire Tragedy provides support for the perception that groupthink may have been a significant factor. However, since Neck et al. (1996) had prior familiarity with the theoretical principles associated with groupthink, Godwin and Neck (1996) argue that their analysis may have been biased towards a conclusion of groupthink, based upon their projection of various attributes of the individuals involved. Therefore, Neck et al. (1996) may have 'fitted' the data to meet with their expectations to explain the events that led to the tragedy.

In contrast to unconscious projection, conscious projection occurs with the full awareness of the researcher (Kahn, 1996). Typically, it involves the projection of one's own attitudes and/or perceptions to another individual. According to Godwin and Neck (1996), an integrated view of both unconscious and conscious projection leads to the following conclusions regarding the impact of projection on research involving case studies:

1. Researchers may project their own beliefs, attitudes and/or behaviour to supplement missing data;
2. Projection can occur with or without the awareness of the researcher; and
3. Prior assumptions or knowledge provide the basis from which projection arises.

While projection is always likely to occur at some level in subjective data analysis, the impact of projection bias can be minimised through the use of independent reviewers and an understanding of the nature of projection amongst researchers.

6.11.4   Ceiling and Floor Effects

Ceiling and floor effects occur when a dependent (measured) variable does not provide for the range of responses that can occur. For example, a test in which most students score 100 percent is not necessarily providing an accurate indication of the differences that exist between individual students. Likewise, a test in which most students score zero will also restrict the extent to which individual comparisons can be made.

Where restrictions in the range of performance occur at the higher end of performance, this is referred to as a 'ceiling effect'. In contrast, where the restriction occurs at the lower end of the performance spectrum, this is referred to as a 'floor effect' (Mitchell & Jolley, 1992).

Ceiling and floor effects occur due to either the characteristics of the dependent measure, and/or the nature of research environment. In the case of the former, the restriction is generally due to a limited number of available options. For example, the awards 'pass' or 'fail' tend to restrict the options such that there is no distinction between individuals within either classification. Where a range of performance levels is required, it may be possible to divide each of these classifications and provide additional options.

Ceiling and floor effects relating to the research environment include noise, interruptions and/or an experimental procedure that is too difficult for participants to complete successfully. One of the most effective means to ameliorate the impact of these effects requires that researchers conduct a preliminary evaluation and seek advice from participants concerning their perceptions of the research study. This provides an opportunity to identify any difficulties that may have been encountered, and which may impact upon the data.

6.11.5 *Serial-Order Effect*

The serial-order effect tends to occur during sequential series of trials in which differences emerge between the responses to trials administrated earlier in the sequence and trials administered later in the sequence. This type of experimental bias may be due to a number of factors including fatigue and practice.

Box 6.1

The serial-order effect

In our study on the effects of alcohol on flying performance, we might test the participants using two different simulation scenarios in sequence: (a) and (b). If we keep the sequence consistent for all participants, the results from (a) might be expected to influence the results in the subsequent trial (b). Therefore, we need to counterbalance the order of scenarios so that the effects of fatigue and/or practice are spread evenly across both scenarios.

In practice, we would expose half the participants to scenario (a) in the first instance, while the other half would be exposed to scenario (b) first. This would ensure that the influence of practice and/or fatigue is equal across conditions.

In terms of the design of questionnaires, the serial-order effect is observed when responses to items included later in a questionnaire are influenced by items that appear in an earlier section. Steinberg (1994) suggests that this type of the serial-order effect may be due to respondents narrowing their attention towards the particular construct under investigation, rather than interpreting each question independently. However, this effect may also be due to fatigue, particularly when the questionnaire comprises a large number of items.

The main outcome of the serial-order effect is a difference between the items answered during the earlier stage of a series of trials, and those answered during later stages. However, this can be overcome by ensuring that the sequence in which the trials are administered is either random or is counterbalanced across respondents. These strategies will also minimise the impact of practice or any fatigue that may occur as the trials progress.

6.11.6 Social Desirability

Social desirability occurs when participants search for the responses that they consider will 'please' the researcher. This is a particularly common response in situations where researchers are familiar with the participants. Consequently, it is important to establish whether social desirability is likely to occur, and develop strategies to minimise the impact on the data. This might include the development of a research design in which the research question or hypothesis is not obvious to the participants.

6.11.7 Questioning Techniques

Questionnaires and surveys are amongst the most prevalent means of data acquisition in social science research. However, the efficacy of these measures is intrinsically dependent upon the type of question asked and, in particular, upon question framing.

Generally, questions included in a questionnaire are presumed to be related to a particular construct such as a dimension of personality, or an attitude or belief. However, Loftus and Palmer (1974) have demonstrated that the type of question asked of a participant can have a significant impact upon the response provided, irrespective of the construct under investigation. They selected a series of seven film clips involving collisions between motor vehicles and showed each film to 45 participants. The participants were subsequently asked to answer a series of questions, the most significant of which was 'About how fast were the cars going when they _____ each other?' The words used to complete the sentence were either 'smashed', 'collided', 'bumped', 'hit' or 'contacted'.

According to Loftus and Palmer (1974), the results indicated that where the word 'smashed' was used, the estimated collision speed was significantly greater than when the word 'collided' was used. This, in turn, was greater than when the term 'bumped' was employed in the sentence. One week later, those participants in the group in which 'smashed' was used reported the presence of broken glass when, in fact, there was no broken glass in the original film.

Leading questions of the type employed by Loftus and Palmer (1974) are not easy to avoid, and it behoves the researcher to consider the nature of the questions asked, prior to implementation. In addition, measuring tools should be used that have been subjected to checks of reliability, validity and norms. Finally, Mitchell and Jolley (1992) suggest that researchers should ensure that the questions included in questionnaires or surveys:

- Be free of jargon and written at a level appropriate for the population under investigation;
- Avoid the use of words that may be subject to misinterpretation;
- Seek personal information only if necessary;
- Offer alternatives, rather than lead the respondent to a particular response;
- Avoid the use of questions that contain an element of social desirability;
- Avoid questions with more than one subject;
- Be short and to the point;
- Are relevant; and
- Avoid the use of double negatives.

In terms of simplifying the structure of questions, Bordens and Abbott (1991) suggest that words containing more than seven letters may be substituted with less complex terminology. This is designed to facilitate the accurate and efficient interpretation of questions amongst respondents and, therefore, provide a firm foundation for the acquisition of appropriate data.

The specificity of questions also reduces the extent to which they should be subject to interpretation. For example, the sentence:

> How many times in the last year did you
> experience an in-flight passenger disturbance?

may be interpreted as the number of events in the previous calendar year, or the number of events in the previous year to date. Consequently, a more specific question is necessary such as:

> How many times in 1997 did you experience
> an in-flight passenger disturbance?

This reduces the ambiguity of the question and, thereby, increases the accuracy of the responses.

In some cases, responses will be sought to questions for which there is a morally or socially desirable response. For example, the question 'Do you think that the airlines of emerging nations are unsafe and corrupt?' suggests to the respondent that there is a 'correct' or 'appropriate' response. Therefore, the response is open to the influence of social desirability, in which a respondent seeks acceptance by choosing the 'correct' answer, rather than examining the question on its merits. An alternative question might be 'What is your first impression of airlines from nations such as ...?'.

Clearly, questionnaire design is a balance between specificity and ambiguity on the one hand, and complexity and simplicity on the other. A questionnaire that is too vague or broad may not elicit the appropriate type of data required to examine a particular construct. Similarly, a questionnaire that is too specific may lead to responses that are highly regimented, and which do not reflect the complexity of human values and beliefs.

An alternative to designing a novel questionnaire involves the adaptation or direct application of an existing questionnaire or survey. References to existing questionnaires are usually found in previous research, although copies of the instruments are rarely included in the publication. Some questionnaires are subject to copyright provisions and must be purchased from a publisher (such as the Myers-Briggs Type Indicator or MBTI). In addition, prospective researchers may be required to attend a workshop pertaining to the appropriate administration and interpretation of the questionnaire. For those questionnaires that do not need to be purchased (such as the Flight Management Attitudes Questionnaire), good practice demands that permission be sought from the author/s prior to the administration of the instrument. Finally, some questionnaires or tests may only be administered by a registered psychologist.

6.12 Chapter Summary

This chapter examined some of the issues involved in conducting social science research in the aviation environment. An initial examination of the aviation industry revealed several issues that characterise social science research in aviation. In particular, aviation represents a relatively attractive research environment because of the opportunities afforded by high technology, the consequences of system failures, and the role that aviation plays in the world economy.

Some of the more practical aspects associated with social science research were also considered including funding limitations, time constraints, and the desire for applied outcomes that can be implemented immediately. This discussion provided the basis for a consideration of the extent and availability of industry support and the mechanisms involved in seeking assistance, particularly in terms of potential participants.

The principles of research planning were examined in the context of limited resources and time constraints. It was shown that the research plan will be dependent upon the characteristics of the research setting, and a number of strategies were considered to facilitate the efficient and effective application of resources.

Research bias is a significant factor that may reduce the accuracy of the data acquired during social science research. A number of biases were identified including the Hawthorne, halo, and serial-order effects. In each case, strategies were suggested to minimise the impact of these biases. Ultimately, the researcher needs to consider whether the results obtained are due to the manipulation of the independent variable, or whether they are an experimental artefact.

The final section of this chapter considered the more applied aspects of questioning techniques including an analysis of the principles of effective question design, and questionnaire development.

6.13   Further Reading

Anastasi, A. (1988). *Psychological testing* (6th ed.). New York, NY: Macmillan.

Bouma, G.D. (1995). *The research process.* Melbourne, AUS: Oxford University Press.

Hedrick, T.E., Bickman, L., & Rog, D.J. (1993). *Applied research design: A practical guide.* Newbury Park, CA: Sage.

Kirk, R.E. (1968). *Experimental design: Procedures for the behavioural sciences.* Belmont, CA: Brooks/Cole.

Kumar, R. (1996). *Research methodology.* Sydney, AUS: Longman.

Leach, J. (1991). *Running applied psychology experiments.* Bristol, PA: Open University Press.

McGuigan, F.J. (1997). *Experimental psychology: Methods of research* (7th ed.). New Jersey, NJ: Prentice Hall.

7   Introduction to Quantitative Data Analysis

7.1   Introduction

Data analysis represents the penultimate stage of the research process. Having acquired the data as accurately and as reliably as possible, the researcher is charged with making sense of the information such that conclusions can be drawn with respect to the research question or hypothesis.

This chapter examines a number of general principles of quantitative data analysis including the notions of reliability and validity, and the use of the measures of central tendency to describe data. These principles provide the basis for a detailed consideration of qualitative and quantitative forms of data analysis and interpretation. The underlying assumptions are described, in addition to some of the key strategies involved in the application of these techniques for data analysis.

It should be noted that there are detailed and specialised texts available on all aspects of research design and methodology including experimental studies, survey and questionnaire design, and case studies, as well as textbooks on the theory and application of statistical techniques. Although some of the basic principles of data analysis are introduced here, it is recommended that texts dedicated to this area be consulted once the basic principles have been grasped. A list of introductory and more advanced texts can be found at the end of this chapter.

As a part of the discussion concerning qualitative and quantitative forms of data analysis, the advantages and disadvantages of each approach are considered in detail. In particular, researchers should be aware that these strategies for data analysis begin from very different perspectives, and are designed to yield different types of information that may or may not be relevant to the initial research question.

7.2   The Importance of Significance Testing

Data analysis is the primary means by which researchers can establish reasoned responses to research questions and hypotheses. Unfortunately, the process of data analysis is often perceived as an arduous task that is both difficult and confusing, particularly amongst inexperienced researchers. However, data analysis need not be a difficult process, and very simple comparisons have the potential to yield important results. For example, an inspection of fatal aircraft accident occurrences amongst scheduled passenger operations indicates that during the period 1977-1981, a total of 33 percent of accidents were beyond the control of the crew, in comparison with 67 percent during the period 1992-1996 (Bruggink, 1998). This relatively simple observation provides some useful information concerning the changing nature of aircraft accident causation.

A major part of the process of data analysis involves deciding which type of analytical strategy to employ. Generally, the choice of strategy will be dependent upon the nature of the research question, the type of data available and the research environment. Consequently, it is important for researchers to consider the process of data analysis *prior* to the acquisition of data.

In broad terms, data analytical techniques are generally divided according to the type of data involved. For example, qualitative techniques are applied when data are non-numeric, such as the response to an open-ended question. In contrast, quantitative techniques are applied when the data are numeric, such as the score on an examination, or the airspeed of an aircraft. Irrespective of the type of analytical technique employed, the accuracy of any analytical process will depend on two important characteristics associated with the nature of the data: reliability and validity.

7.3   Reliability

Data are said to be reliable if, given the same environment and the same stimulus, consistent data are recorded over repeated trials (Bryman & Cramer, 1994; Hunter & Burke, 1994). Consistent results suggest that there are no confounding variables that are likely to impact upon the data, such that they influence one participant and not another.

For example, if the data arising from a questionnaire are dependent upon the time at which it is completed, the completion of the questionnaire at different times will yield different results. Unless this confounding factor is taken into account during the process of data acquisition, the results may be erroneous.

In the first instance, ensuring the reliability of data can be accomplished during research planning, where potential confounding factors are taken into account and/or eliminated. For example, a structured interview might need to be conducted at a time when participants have an opportunity to consider the questions without interruption. This may require some flexibility and/or preplanning on the part of both the researcher and the participant/s. However, this strategy also reduces the extent to which the results may be due to the particular circumstances under which the responses were elicited.

In addition to the research environment, research materials may also have an influence on the data acquired, particularly if a question is ambiguous and subject to interpretation (Klein, Calderwood, & MacGregor, 1989). Therefore, it may be necessary to pretest a questionnaire and/or interview protocol using a small subgroup of the population from which the sample will be drawn. This 'pilot' study provides an opportunity to gain useful information prior to data acquisition with a view towards increasing the reliability of the data.

7.3.1   Types of Reliability

The reliability of a survey or questionnaire is defined as the extent to which each of the questions/statements is free from non-systematic errors which may bias responses (Aiken, 1979). These errors tend to arise when there is a level of ambiguity or inconsistency associated with a question, such that the responses tend to vary according to factors such as the time of day, or the process of administration. The difficulty associated with these factors is that it is impossible to predict the extent to which they impact upon the responses.

A common method of establishing reliability involves the administration of the same questionnaire on two separate occasions. This is referred to as the test-retest method, and is designed to determine the extent to which responses remain consistent over time. Where a particular construct is assumed to be stable over time, reliability is assumed to exist when respondents interpret the questions pertaining to that construct in the same way during each administration of a questionnaire. It is the most powerful way to analyse the impact of non-systematic errors and to determine what is referred to as the level of external consistency.

In addition to external consistency, internal consistency is another important element associated with reliability, since most questionnaires include a series of different questions that are all designed to examine the same construct or underlying dimension. Internal consistency refers to the extent to which the responses to each question are related, given that they are designed to examine the same construct. Typically, an overall score is computed for each particular element of the questionnaire, and a comparison is made between the mean values.

The split-half method is a common mechanism to determine internal consistency, and this involves dividing those items that are designed to examine a single construct into two sets. The responses from each set are then compared. Given that the questionnaire is reliable, it would be expected that, as the responses to one set change, the responses to the other set will change in direct proportion.

7.4   Validity

The validity of data is the extent to which the data acquired is an accurate measure of the variable under investigation (Christensen, 1991; Goldstein, 1978). For example, a positive response to the statement 'my organisation has an appropriate level of system safety' may be either a reflection of loyalty to the organisation, a reflection of the fear of recrimination, and/or an accurate reflection of the perception of system safety within the organisation. However, the nature of the question is such that it is not possible to determine which of these factors was most salient in the response.

In terms of measuring instruments, there are a number of different types of validity, the simplest of which is *face validity*. In this case, the types of questions asked are examined to determine whether they appear to be measuring an appropriate dimension.

For example, suppose that a researcher intends to develop a personality inventory to predict the performance of air traffic controllers. From previous research, it is understood that there are a number of distinct skills and capabilities required by an air traffic controller, including:

- The ability to relate two dimensions to three dimensions;

- The ability to manage stress;
- The ability to communicate effectively;
- The ability to work as a member of a team;
- The ability to obtain information from a number of distinct sources;
- The ability to anticipate; and
- The ability to prioritise (Schneider, 1985).

It can be assumed for the purposes of this example, that these abilities reflect an underlying set of personality characteristics. For example, an individual with a relatively wide social network is more likely to be able to function as part of a team, than a person who is unable to form relationships. On the basis of this belief, a series of questions and/or statements might be developed that are designed to assess this dimension.

When assessing personality, respondents are typically asked to read a particular statement and determine the extent to which it reflects their own attitudes or behaviour. For example, consider the following:

Please circle the response which best reflects your personal behaviour in relation to the following statement.

I prefer to play team games more than individual sports.

Strongly Agree	Agree	No Preference	Disagree	Strongly Disagree

In the case of this example, the face validity of the question would be examined by determining the extent to which the question appears to be assessing the dimension 'ability to work as part of a team'. There is no other means of testing face validity than its appearance with respect to the dimension being examined (Aiken, 1979). Consequently, this is the least accurate of the measures of validity.

In contrast, *construct validity* is a more analytical and laborious process. Construct validity is the degree to which a particular test or assessment is actually measuring the construct that it was designed to measure. For example, a test may have been devised to examine the construct 'pilot leadership', since leadership skills are presumed to be a factor in the success of pilots during command training. In this case, determining the construct validity of a test of leadership would involve an analysis of test scores in situations in which the construct is expected to be particularly evident. Therefore, it might be expected that pilots who have obtained their captaincy should score at a higher level than their contemporaries who have not reached this level, since leadership characteristics are expected to play a significant role in promotion.

Allied to the notion of construct validity is *predictive validity* or the extent to which a test is predictive of a particular outcome. Returning to the previous example concerning the selection of air traffic controllers, it might be expected that a relationship would exist between scores on the initial selection test, and performance as an air traffic controller following selection.

Undoubtedly, the capability to predict future performance is the primary goal associated with the development of selection and testing procedures within the aviation environment. However, there is some difficulty in determining which types of procedures are most appropriate in aviation and, indeed, what level of relationship can be expected. Hunter and Burke (1994) conducted a meta-analysis of 68 pilot selection studies and found that the mean validity was relatively small for most of the predictors of pilot performance, including verbal ability, spatial ability, age, education and personality. This does not necessarily suggest that all pilot selection procedures are ineffective. Rather, it indicates that some techniques may be more effective than others under certain conditions and for specific populations. The advantage of measuring predictive validity is that it provides an estimate of confidence concerning the accuracy of a measure.

A useful rule of thumb in conducting social science research that employs a series of questionnaires is to use, where possible, existing measuring instruments. The instruction manual that accompanies the test will include measures of reliability and validity, and population norms for the test. These can be used to guide the administration of the test and the interpretation of the data (see Chapter 6: Section 6.11.7).

7.5 Quantitative Data Analysis

Statistical analysis is becoming more and more an integral part of the aviation industry, from analyses of profit margins to investigations associated with aircraft accidents. Consequently, it is important for practitioners to develop the skills necessary to interpret and communicate statistical information accurately and effectively.

Statistics can be thought of as a language that must be learnt and practised if the user is to become a fluent communicator. Like any other language, statistics is designed to convey meaning and facilitate some level of understanding. Specifically, the language is designed to derive meaning from a wide variety of data sources, either related or unrelated. However, the difficulty associated with statistics is that the relative value of the information is dependent upon the quality of the interpretation. Statistics and statistical analyses should be regarded as tools that illustrate and provide a justification for conclusions. As the saying goes: 'Statistics can be both used and abused', and clever statistics will not fix a poor research design.

As a hypothetical example illustrating the importance of accurate interpretation, consider the situation in which the total number of aircraft accidents during one year decreased in comparison to the previous year. Questions should arise as to whether the decrease was:

a)   Greater than would have occurred purely by chance; and/or

b)   Indicative of an increase in overall safety.

These questions are fundamental to the aviation industry in terms of future policy directions and/or funding allocations. However, the answers to these questions can only be determined through an analysis of the statistics arising from the accident data.

In answer to question (a), it must be assumed that, within any given year, a random fluctuation will occur in terms of the number of accidents that are reported. For example, 1985 was a particularly poor year in terms of the number of fatalities involving scheduled passenger airlines over 27,000kg (see Figure 7.1). In isolation, this result might have been perceived as indicative of a sudden decrease in safety amongst scheduled passenger airlines.

However, taken together with the statistics for fatalities in 1984 and 1986, there is evidence to suggest that the result in 1985 might have been due to a statistical aberration that occurred simply through chance. For example, in 1986, there were only 57 fatalities amongst scheduled airline services (Oster, Strong & Zorn. 1992). Therefore, for every bad year in terms of aircraft accidents, there are also very good years that tend to counteract the overall effect. This is a statistical pattern that is referred to as 'regression to the mean'. It reflects the distribution of a random series of events, and suggests that a single occurrence, taken in isolation, is not necessarily indicative of the broad nature of a particular construct.

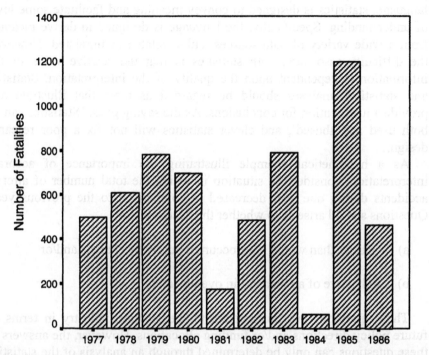

Figure 7.1 Number of fatalities worldwide for aircraft over 27,000kg for the years 1977 through 1986 (adapted from Oster et al. 1992)

In terms of identifying an 'actual' decline in aviation safety, it is more appropriate to examine events during the years prior to 1985 to determine whether a change has occurred. This provides a long-term trend, the use of which is more reliable than basing judgements on the results of a relatively limited series of events. In the case of aviation safety, evidence of a decrease might be characterised by a relatively consistent trend in which a change occurs over a period of time.

The application of statistics more generally is dependent upon 'trends' and, therefore, it is important to acquire a sample of data, rather than simply infer information on the basis of a single data point. Certainly, an inspection of an isolated event, such as an aircraft accident, may reveal some useful information. However, it may not be possible to draw meaningful conclusions or make long-term predictions.

7.6   Statistics and Aviation Safety

As indicated in the previous section, aviation safety is a term that is often difficult to define and, therefore, can be difficult to analyse. Even the frequency of aircraft accidents is a somewhat simplistic measure, since a decline in accidents may simply have resulted from fewer hours being flown, due perhaps to a recession or an increase in oil prices.

A more accurate means of assessment might involve the number of aircraft accidents divided by the total number of hours flown during a given period. This is referred to as the 'accident rate' and it is widely regarded as the primary means of measuring aviation safety retrospectively (Wiener, 1993). Variations to this assessment technique include:

a) $\text{Passenger Miles} = \dfrac{\text{Number of Passengers}}{\text{Number of Miles Flown}}$

b) $\text{Passenger Flight Miles} = \dfrac{\text{Number of Passengers}}{\text{Number of Passengers for a Given Distance}}$

Although there is some dispute as to the most appropriate means of measuring aviation safety, the main guideline is that comparisons should be made using a consistent frame of reference (Laudan, 1994). Irrespective of the measure used, maintaining the frame of reference should be sufficient to reveal any substantive changes over a given period.

7.7   Descriptive Statistics in Aviation Research

Possibly the most important differentiation made between the various statistical dialects is that between the terms 'inferential' and 'descriptive' statistics. It is an important difference since inferential and descriptive statistics have distinctive properties that may lead to differing conclusions being drawn.

Descriptive statistics are used to describe the nature of data. They comprise a number of general measures including measures of central tendency, such as the mean, median and mode, and measures of the dispersion of scores, such as the standard deviation and variance. These measures effectively summarise a set of data into a single descriptive value that reflects the general nature of the data set.

7.7.1 Mean

The mean (or average) is the most common statistic used to describe large amounts of data and provide a measure of central tendency (Spatz & Johnston, 1989). It can be calculated by summing a series of values and subsequently dividing by the total number of values in the series (see Example 7.1).

Example 7.1

The mean is designed to summarise either interval or ratio data, such as age or hours experience. In the case of hours experience, a trainer might be interested in determining the mean level of experience amongst pilots attending a training course. This information might assist the trainer to deliver the training material at an appropriate level. The data set below lists each participant in the course and their associated level of experience in terms of total hours flown.

Data Set	Participant No.	Experience (hrs)
	1	2,300
	2	6,500
	3	2,600
	4	2,300
	5	900

The formula for the mean is depicted as:

Equation to calculate the mean

$$\overline{X} = \frac{\sum X}{n}$$

where:

$\overline{X}$ = symbolic representation of the arithmetic mean;

$\sum X$ = sum of all the values available; and

n = number of values available

Results for Example 7.1

$$\overline{X} = \frac{\sum X}{n} =$$

$$\frac{2,300 + 12,500 + 2,600 + 2,300 + 900}{5} = 4,120 \text{ hours}$$

In the case of Example 7.1, the mean experience of pilots involved in training course is 4,120 hours. However, it should be noted that this value incorporates a pilot with 12,500 hours experience and a pilot with 900 hours experience. This could present problems for the trainer, since the material is being delivered at a level appropriate for pilots with approximately 4,000 (4,120) hours.

7.7.2   Median

The median is an alternative to the mean, and is used when the mid-point is required for a series of ranked data (Sommer & Sommer, 1980). This is often used in cases where there are outliers evident in a range of scores within a particular series, or if the data are ordinal. Consider Example 7.1 and the observation that, although the experience of a majority of pilots was below 2,500 hours, the mean level experience was calculated as 4,120 hours. This was due primarily to the influence of Data Point 2, since this value was substantially greater than the majority. Indeed, the use of the mean may have led to an erroneous perception of pilot experience in this situation. In cases where outlying data are evident, the median often represents a more appropriate measure of central tendency, since the mean is influenced by extreme scores (see Example 7.2).

Example 7.2

Using a data set identical to that in Example 7.1, the series is ranked from least to highest and the middle value is taken as representative of the overall series.

Data Set	Participant No.	Experience (hrs)
	5	900
	4	2,300
(Mid-score = Median value)	1	2,300
	3	2,600
	2	12,500

Having ranked the data, it is possible to determine the mid-score. This score is referred to as the median and, in this case, the value is 2,300 hours. It is now possible to develop a more accurate summary of the level of experience amongst the majority of participants involved the training course.

Note the differences between the values obtained using the mean and the median, and note which is more likely to represent an accurate measure of central tendency.

7.7.3 Mode

The mode is the least preferred measure of central tendency, and involves the identification of the observation that occurs most frequently within the data set (see Example 7.3). It is particularly difficult to develop valid and reliable conclusions using the mode, although it can be useful as a summary measure in some cases (Sommer & Sommer, 1980).

Example 7.3

Using the following data set, the mode is calculated by noting the observation that occurs most frequently.

Data Set No.	Experience (hrs)
1	2,300
2	12,500
3	2,600
4	2,300
5	900

In this case, the mode has a value of 2,300 hours, since it occurs in both Data Points 1 and 4. Since no other value occurs more than once, the value 2,300 has the greatest frequency of occurrence in the data set.

Clearly, measures of central tendency are useful descriptors of the nature of a particular data set. They allow the researcher to get a general feel for the data with the reduction of the data set to a single, descriptive value. However, they do not provide all of the information necessary for a comprehensive comparison between groups that is often necessary in aviation-related analysis. This is due to the fact that differences between measures of central tendency may or may not reflect actual differences that exist between groups. For example, consider two sets of fictional test scores where one set contains the values 2, 2, 2 and the other set consists of scores 1, 1, 4. The mean of both these groups is exactly the same (2). Yet it is apparent that the *dispersion* of the scores in the two groups is quite different. On its own, the mean is uninformative and there is generally a requirement for a measure of the dispersion, or what is referred to as the standard deviation. The standard deviation provides a basis for assessing the meaning of a score in relation to other scores. For example, a researcher might be interested in whether a particular score is above or below the mean, and by how many units of standard deviation it differs from the mean. The result will provide an indication of the extent to which a score is typical compared with other scores from the same sample.

Many statistical tests take into account the dispersion of scores in measuring whether the mean scores for groups differ significantly from each other in a statistical sense. This concept is considered in more detail in Section 7.7.5 and Chapter 8.

Box 7.1

Descriptive statistics

Imagine that we have conducted our experiment concerning the effect of blood alcohol level on pilot performance. At this stage, we might simply be interested in determining the effect of alcohol on performance, irrespective of other factors such as age or sex. The dependent variable was a measure of deviation in degrees while following the glide-slope on an Instrument Landing System (ILS). In this case, our experimental hypothesis was that performance would be poorer under conditions of moderate alcohol intake, relative to low and no alcohol intake. The task was undertaken in a flight simulator and the deviations were recorded over a twenty-second period both prior to (baseline), and after the ingestion of the prescribed amount of alcohol. For simplicity, we will consider the scores recorded during the post-treatment test.

Having collated the deviation from each participant in each group, we need to describe the general pattern in the results.

The means of three groups (These deviations would be calculated using the average deviation, irrespective of the direction):

No alcohol:	.04 degrees deviation
Low alcohol:	0.9 degrees deviation
Moderate alcohol:	1.3 degrees deviation

Immediately, we can see that this measure of central tendency suggests a pattern of scores that is consistent with our hypothesis: performance is poorest (greater degrees deviation) in the moderate alcohol condition. Inferential statistics are required to measure whether the apparent differences reflected in the means can be regarded as truly or significantly different from one another.

7.7.4   *Frequency Distributions*

Frequency distributions are useful for displaying data in a graphic form, and for determining the characteristics associated with a range of the scores (see Example 7.4).

Example 7.4

Consider two data sets, one of which relates to the age of pilots involved in accidents resulting from a failure to lower the undercarriage, and the other relating to the age of pilots involved in accidents resulting from fuel starvation. The aim of this comparison is to determine whether any differences exist between the average age of pilots involved in these types of aircraft accidents.

Data Set 1 Participant No.	Age	Data Set 2 Participant No.	Age
1	31	1	45
2	46	2	34
3	47	3	71
4	32	4	65
5	37	5	54
6	48	6	30
7	57	7	32
8	36	8	33
9	56	9	25
10	38	10	25

The first step in the process of developing a frequency distribution is to create a tally of the frequency of occurrences for each category. For example, in the case of Data Set 1 in Example 7.4, a tally of the frequency of occurrences for a series of age groups would yield:

Age Group (Years)	Tally (Frequency)
15-25	0
26-35	2
36-45	3
46-55	3
56-65	2
66-75	0

These data can now be plotted on a graph where the height of the column reflects the relative number of occurrences (see Figure 7.2). In this example, the distribution of values is clustered symmetrically about the mean to form a normal distribution, also known as a 'bell' curve. The majority of random events will conform to a normal distribution. For example, the distribution of the height of Licensed Aircraft Mechanical Engineers (LAME) within a particular organisation would probably approximate a normal distribution if the data were plotted on a histogram. A similar effect could be expected for the frequency of different body weights or scores on intelligence tests, given that the LAMEs represent a random sample.

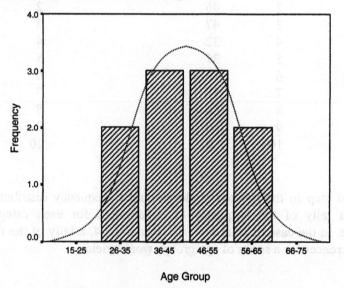

Figure 7.2 A histogram, illustrating the distribution of scores from Data Set 1 in Example 7.4

The pattern of the distribution of test scores or data points is important when considering the application of statistical analyses. In many cases, statistical analyses can only be used if the distribution of data conforms to a normal distribution. However, there are many cases in which the distribution of data does not conform to a normal distribution.

Where a pattern of scores is clustered at the higher or lower end of a frequency distribution, the pattern is said to be skewed. Figure 7.3 presents an example of a positively skewed distribution, based upon the scores in Data Set 2 from Example 7.4. In this case, the scores are clustered at the lower end of the distribution and the tail or skew is at the positive (right) end of the dimension. By contrast, a negatively skewed distribution is said to exist when the scores are clustered at the higher end of a frequency distribution and the tail is at the negative (left) end of the dimension.

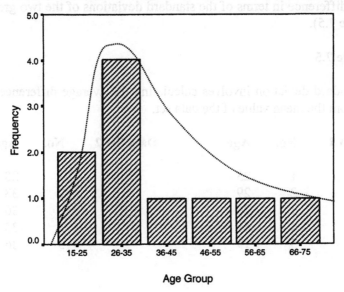

Figure 7.3 A histogram, illustrating the distribution of scores from Data Set 2 in Example 7.4

It should be noted that the mean value for both Data Sets 1 and 2 in Example 7.4, is 42.8. This occurs despite the fact that the distribution, or dispersion of values in the two sets is quite different. Therefore, prior to drawing any conclusions regarding the similarities or differences between data sets, it is important to consider the dispersion of scores within each group. This requires the consideration of the standard deviation and the variance of the scores.

7.7.5 Standard Deviation

Although the standard deviation is classified as a descriptive statistic, it is not a measure of central tendency. Simply defined, it is the average deviation of the scores from the mean value of the data set (Bryman & Cramer, 1994). Therefore, it is a measure of the spread of scores, or the extent to which a group of scores differs from the mean, and it is important as a measure of variability or dispersion.

In Example 7.4, note that the scores in Data Set 1 differed from the mean to a greater extent than those scores in Data Set 2. Therefore, there is likely to be a difference in terms of the standard deviations of the two groups (see Example 7.5).

Example 7.5

The standard deviation involves calculating the average difference of each score from the mean value of the data set.

Data Set 1	No.	Age	Data Set 2	No.	Age
	1	23		1	28
	2	29		2	33
	3	26		3	30
	4	65		4	35
	5	19		5	36

The formula is depicted as:

**Equation to calculate
the standard deviation
(sample of population)**

$$s = \sqrt{\frac{\sum X^2 - \dfrac{(\sum X)^2}{N}}{N-1}}$$

where:

$\sum X^2$ = the sum of the squared scores;

$(\sum X)^2$ = the square of the sum of the raw scores; and

N = the number of scores

Data Set #1

$$s = \sqrt{\frac{(529 + 841 + 676 + 4225 + 361) - \dfrac{(162)^2}{5}}{4}} =$$

$$s = \sqrt{\frac{(23^2 + 29^2 + 26^2 + 65^2 + 19^2) - \dfrac{(23 + 29 + 26 + 65 + 19)^2}{5}}{4}} =$$

$$s = \sqrt{\frac{6632 - \dfrac{26244}{5}}{4}} = 18.60$$

Data Set #2

$$s = \sqrt{\frac{5294 - \dfrac{26244}{5}}{4}} = 3.36$$

Variable	Mean	Standard Deviation	Min Value	Max Value	N (Scores)
Age (1)	32.4	*18.60*	19	65	5
Age (2)	32.4	*3.36*	28	36	5

Although the two means are identical for these data sets, the standard deviations are quite different (18.6 versus 3.36). Therefore, it can be assumed that the spread of the scores is different. This is yet another method to describe the characteristics of a particular population or sample. In addition, the square of the standard deviation, referred to as *variance*, is an important component for statistical analyses in which inferences are made about the characteristics of a population (see Section 8.5.3).

7.8   Chapter Summary

The aim of this chapter was to introduce some of the fundamental concepts that provide the basis for the analysis of quantitative data. In particular, the chapter included an outline of the principles of reliability and validity as a precursor to the process of data analysis. Furthermore, the use and potential misuse of statistical information was discussed, both within the aviation environment and within other domains.

The main part of the chapter involved a consideration of descriptive techniques of data analysis within social science research. These included measures of central tendency including the mean, median and mode, and the calculation of the standard deviation as it might be applied to social science research in aviation. These statistics can be used to describe the characteristics of the sample and the data sets, and provide a useful step in the initial inspection of results.

7.9   Further Reading

Anastasi, A. (1988). *Psychological testing* (6th ed.). New York, NY: Macmillan.

Bryman, A., & Cramer, C. (1994). *Quantitative data analysis for social scientists*. London, UK: Routledge.

Howell, D.C. (1997). *Statistical methods for psychology* (4th ed.). Belmont, CA: Duxbury Press.

Kirk, R.E. (1968). *Experimental design: Procedures for the behavioural sciences.* Belmont, CA: Brooks/Cole.

McGuigan, F.J. (1997). *Experimental psychology: Methods of research* (7th ed.). New Jersey, NJ: Prentice Hall.

Minium, E.W., King, B.M., & Bear, G. (1993). *Statistical reasoning in psychology and education* (3rd ed.). New York, NY: Wiley.

Rowntree, D. (1991). *Statistics without tears: A primer for non-mathematicians.* London, UK: Penguin.

Siegel, S., & Castellan, N.J. (1988). *Non-parametric statistics for the behavioural sciences* (2nd ed.). New York, NY: McGraw-Hill.

Spatz, C., & Johnston, J.O. (1989). *Basic statistics: Tales of distributions.* Pacific Grove, CA: Brooks/Cole.

Winer, B.J. (1971). *Statistical principles in experimental design* (2nd ed.). New York, NY: McGraw-Hill.

8   Inferential Statistics in Aviation Research

8.1   Introduction

Inferential statistics are used to infer information about a population from a subset or sample of that population (Spatz & Johnston, 1989). Therefore, the first question that must be asked as part of any inferential technique is whether or not the results obtained are likely to be indicative of the population from which the sample was drawn. If the answer is in the affirmative, conclusions can be made concerning the particular relationships or differences between the various conditions or groups.

For example, in one group of pilots, an accident rate might be observed that is higher than that observed in another group. Further analysis may reveal differences in terms of age, with younger pilots more likely to be represented in the accident statistics. However, this does not necessarily indicate that these pilots are representative of all young pilots, since the pilots in the sample may also be relatively inexperienced. Therefore, the sample may be more representative of the population of inexperienced pilots, independent of age, rather than of the population of younger pilots as a whole.

Inferential statistics are generally used to compare or contrast groups defined by the researcher to determine whether a difference or relationship between scores is significant from a statistical perspective. A useful rule of thumb when using inferential statistics to compare groups, is that a minimum of 15 data points should be included within each group in a data set. The actual sample size required for a particular analysis can be estimated using the formula for calculating *power*. Generally, the recommended sample size will be dependent upon the estimated size of the effect, and the residual variance (see Kirk, 1968). It is important to consider the assumptions associated with particular statistical analyses, since these will often determine the overall usefulness of the results and the validity of the conclusions that are drawn.

8.2   Populations versus Samples

In many cases, it is impossible to test an entire population, such as all pilots with between 100 and 1,000 hours of flying experience. Statisticians understand these limitations and have calculated revised formulae so that inferences can be made from a subset or sample of the population. Therefore, it is not always necessary to locate an entire population of pilots in order to derive meaningful results concerning their behaviour. These revised analytical techniques are referred to as inferential statistics and they are often the most meaningful and useful statistical analyses available for social science data.

8.3   Test of Statistical Significance

Inferential statistics are based upon the assumption that an inference can be drawn about a population based on the results of a sample (Bryman & Cramer, 1994). More specifically, inferential statistics involve the test of statistical significance to quantify the level of confidence that a conclusion is accurate (Kachigan, 1991). For example, given two sets of data corresponding to two different levels of the independent variable, is it possible to conclude that there is a statistically significant difference between the groups and reject the null hypothesis? Recall that in most studies there is a pair of hypotheses: The null hypothesis and the alternative hypothesis. The study is conducted in attempt to reject the null hypothesis and, thereby, lend support for the alternative hypothesis.

The test for statistical significance is designed to determine the *probability* that a particular value is obtained, given that the null hypothesis is true. For example, a null hypothesis might specify that no difference exists between two groups of pilots in terms of their intelligence. Samples that are drawn from the population will not be identical, and will differ simply by chance. A test of significance allows a researcher to determine the probability of obtaining a difference between the sample means of the two groups, by chance, given that no difference actually exists. Given that the probability of obtaining the sample difference is less than a pre-set criterion when the null hypothesis is true, the null hypothesis can be rejected, thereby lending support to the research hypothesis.

Box 8.1

Statistical significance

Recall that hypothesis-driven research requires the specification of the null and experimental hypotheses and that, technically, the aim is to reject the null hypothesis. In so doing, the researcher provides support (but not proof) of the experimental hypothesis. In the case of our study concerning the effects of alcohol on flying performance, we proposed the experimental hypothesis that flying performance is poorer under conditions of moderate alcohol intake, relative to low and no alcohol intake. Our null hypothesis is that no difference exists between the three experimental groups.

If we were to conduct this study, we would obtain mean performance scores in each of the three conditions. The question is whether the differences between the mean scores are statistically significant. In particular, what is the probability of obtaining these results if the null hypothesis was true? Depending upon the number of tests that we perform, we may set our criterion to .05 to reach statistical significance. Therefore, the probability of the difference occurring, given that the null hypothesis is true, must be less than 1 in 20 (5 in 100).

If the probability value that we obtain is less than .05, we can conclude that the differences observed between the performance of the three groups were such that at least two of three samples were drawn from different populations. Furthermore, if we conducted a methodologically sound study, we can conclude that these populations are defined by the level of alcohol administered, thereby providing implicit support for the experimental hypothesis.

A criterion (α or alpha) accepted by most social scientists is that the probability of obtaining a difference, given that the null hypothesis is true, should be less than .05 (or a probability of one in twenty) before the null hypothesis is rejected. Where multiple inferential tests are employed, this probability level can be adjusted, depending upon the number of tests being performed (see Bryman & Cramer, 1994 for more details). In either case, the criterion should be set prior to data analysis.

All inferential statistics yield a result that can be subjected to a test of statistical significance, where *p* refers to the probability of obtaining a value given that the null hypothesis is true. The resultant probability figure is compared against the criterion. Where a probability value is less than the criterion, this is written as:

$$p < .05 \text{ or } p < .01 \text{ as appropriate}$$

However, it should be recalled that the significance test is an assessment of the probability of an event (Bryman & Cramer, 1994). Therefore, it is not possible to *prove conclusively* that a difference or similarity exists unless the two entire populations, rather than a sample, are examined. This illustrates the need to quantify the confidence or probability in those cases where samples are used. Alternatively, confidence intervals can be calculated as a way to estimate the results (See Howell, 1997).

8.4   Type I and Type II Errors

Despite the 'rule of thumb' adopted by most social scientists in relation to the level of alpha, aviation is one domain in which this decision requires serious consideration. Harris (1991) notes that since the criterion is probabilistic, it is possible for a researcher to make errors. In significance testing, there are two counterpoising factors that may lead to errors. In the first instance, a researcher may accept a difference or relationship as statistically significant when, in fact, it is not (Type I error). The risk of this type of error can be minimised by reducing the criterion level at which statistical significance is reached (.01, rather than .05). However, as the criterion level for statistical significance is reduced, it also increases the risk of rejecting a difference or relationship when, in fact, it exists (Type II error).

To illustrate the importance of this difference, imagine a research study in which it is hypothesised that the accuracy of an approach and landing will differ, depending upon which of two instruments is used to conduct the approach. To test this hypothesis, participants are allocated to one of two groups, and the alpha criterion is set at .05. Therefore, a Type I error is likely to occur less than one in twenty times.

In the case of this study, a Type I error will occur if the results reveal a statistically significant difference between the two instruments when no difference actually exists. Consequently, the researcher will erroneously conclude that the instruments differ in terms of their impact upon performance when, in fact, this may not be the case (See Figure 8.1). However, by reducing the probability of a Type I error, the probability of a Type II error increases. In this case, the results will fail to indicate a difference between the two instruments, when a difference actually exists.

		If the Null Hypothesis is True	If the Null Hypothesis is False
Decision	Reject Null Hypothesis	Error (Type I) $p = \alpha$	Correct $p = 1 - \beta$
	Accept Null Hypothesis	Correct $p = 1 - \alpha$	Error (Type II) $p = \beta$

Figure 8.1   A decision table illustrating the origins of Type I and Type II errors in hypothesis testing

In general, researchers prefer to err on the side of caution and decrease the probability of a Type I error. This strategy increases the probability that any differences or relationships that are observed are an accurate reflection of the effects that actually exist in reality. However, it also increases the probability that differences which actually exist are not observed (Type II error). According to Harris (1991), this strategy poses a particular problem for safety-related research.

In the analysis of the two instruments described previously, it is more likely that a Type II error will occur than a Type I error. Consequently, it is more likely that the researcher will conclude that no difference exists between the performance of two instruments, when this may not be the case. However, the difficulty is that the outcome of this research has significant implications for aviation safety. For example, one instrument may have a deleterious impact upon performance, and this may not be detected, simply due to the size of the criterion for alpha.

On the basis of this argument, safety researchers need to balance the requirement for accuracy (Type I error), with the potential impact of an erroneous result (Type II error). Hence, the dilemma for researchers.

Under normal circumstances, where a statistic does not reach significance, the result is normally only examined to a very limited extent in social science research. However, in aviation safety research, there may be a need to consider results that 'approach significance', but which may not reach the criterion. This will, at least, flag the possibility that a relationship or difference may exist given different methodological or experimental circumstances.

8.5   Degrees of Freedom

Since samples can be of different sizes and since, as the sample size increases, the standard deviation tends to reduce, the result needs to take into account the size of the sample. This is achieved through a consideration of the degrees of freedom within a sample. Degrees of Freedom (*df*) are related to the number of observations made and they describe the number of deviations from the mean that are able to vary. For example, a series of 14 data points indicates that 13 data points are free to vary around the mean while one must remain fixed to ensure that the average deviation from the mean equals zero.

The main implication of the concept of degrees of freedom is that it determines the shape of the distribution of values. As the *df* increases, the standard deviation decreases. Therefore, the dispersion of scores from the mean is smaller.

Generally, most statistical texts will include a table of criterion values for various inferential statistics. These criterion values are listed according to the degrees of freedom, and the level of statistical significance available to the researcher. However, it should be noted that computer-based statistical analyses will normally calculate the degrees of freedom and an absolute level of statistical significance as part of the standard application of an inferential statistical analysis. Nevertheless, it is important to understand the principles upon which these calculations are based.

8.6 Parametric Tests

Inferential statistics fall into one of two categories dependent upon the assumptions that underlie the analysis. For example, statistical analyses such as Analysis of Variance, *t*-test, and the Pearson product-moment correlation are based upon the assumption that the data acquired are samples from a normal frequency distribution with a fixed mean and standard deviation (see Figure 8.2). More importantly, they require that dependent variables be distributed as an interval or ratio scale (see Chapter 3, Section 3.4.8). Recall that interval data consists of a scale wherein the distance between each unit is equidistant, such as age or reaction time.

8.6.1 Correlation

Correlation analyses are among the most common statistical tests employed in social science research within the aviation environment. They are designed to determine the strength of the relationship between two or more variables, and include the Pearson Product-Moment Correlation, the Spearman Correlation, and the Point Biserial Correlation.

A correlation analysis can be employed where a researcher hypothesises that a relationship exists between two or more variables. For example, it might be hypothesised that a relationship exists between pilot experience and aeronautical knowledge. Therefore, the aim of the data analysis is to determine the strength of the relationship between the two variables, 'experience on a type of aircraft' and 'aeronautical knowledge'.

The choice between the various types of correlation analyses is dependent upon the characteristics of the data arising from the research. Where the data are interval or ratio, a Pearson Product-Moment Correlation is generally most appropriate. However, where the data are ordinal or rank-ordered, the Spearman Correlation or Kendall's Tau (τ) may be more appropriate. Finally, where one variable is categorical and the other is continuous, the Point Biserial Correlation can be employed.

Normally, at least one of the two or more variables under investigation must be continuous, such that they have potential to range along a continuum. Height, weight, and age are all examples of continuous variables. They contrast with categorical variables such as sex or occupation where only a distinct number of classifications are possible.

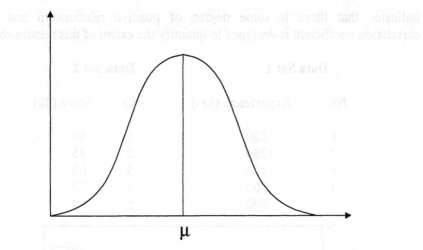

Figure 8.2   An example of a normal distribution. The population mean is indicated in the centre of the curve

As in most forms of statistical analysis, all correlation analyses require that a number of data points be examined. Example 8.1 details the process for calculating a Pearson Product-Moment Correlation Coefficient.

Example 8.1

The Pearson Product-Moment Correlation is designed to determine the extent of the relationship between two or more continuous variables (Bryman & Cramer, 1994). Two fictional data sets are used in this example. The first data set consists of aeronautical experience in the form of hours accumulated. The other data set contains, for each value of experience, an associated percentage score on an aeronautical test. In this case, it might be hypothesised that aeronautical experience is positively related to the scores on the test.

Perusal of these data should indicate a relatively strong relationship between the two data sets. For example, a higher value in Data Set 1 tends to co-relate or correspond with a high value in Data Set 2. This relationship can be illustrated graphically by plotting the two data sets on a graph or scatterplot (see Figure 8.3). It should be noted that the cluster of values approximates a straight line with increasing values. The right-sloping ellipse indicates that there is some degree of positive relationship and the correlation coefficient is designed to quantify the extent of this relationship.

Data Set 1		Data Set 2	
No.	Experience (hrs)	No.	Score (%)
1	130	1	60
2	1280	2	85
3	150	3	63
4	760	4	72
5	500	5	69

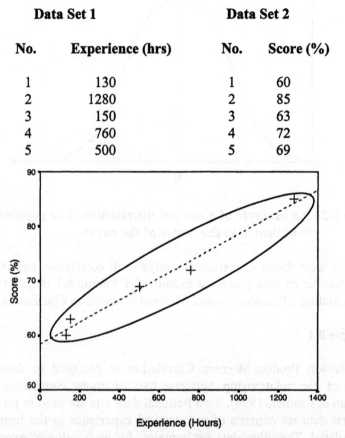

Figure 8.3 Scatter plot illustrating the relationship between percentage scores on an aeronautical test and aeronautical experience (hours)

The formula for the Pearson Product-Moment Correlation Coefficient is:

Equation to Calculate the Pearson Product-Moment Correlation Coefficient (r)

$$r = \frac{\dfrac{\sum XY}{N} - (\overline{X})(\overline{Y})}{(S_x)(S_y)}$$

where: X and Y are paired observations;

XY = the product of each X value multiplied by its paired Y value

$\overline{X}$ = mean value of variable X

$\overline{Y}$ = mean value of variable Y

S_x = standard deviation of variable X

S_y = standard deviation of variable Y

N = number of pairs of observations

Score

Experience	.9902	Correlation Coefficient
	(5)	Pairs of Data Points
	$p = .001$	Probability

The Pearson Product-Moment Correlation can normally be calculated using a standard computer-based statistical package. In the case of Example 8.1, the results are presented in the format produced using the Statistical Package for the Social Sciences (SPSS). The results of this analysis indicate that the correlation coefficient (r) between the variables 'score' and 'experience' is +0.9902, based upon five data points. A coefficient of +1.0 would indicate a perfect, *positive* linear correlation (see Figure 8.4), where an increase in the value of one variable corresponds precisely to a consistent rate of increase in the other variable.

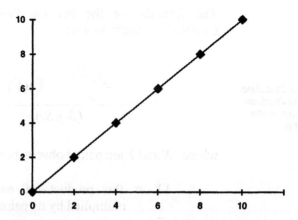

Figure 8.4   An example of a positive linear correlation

In contrast, a correlation coefficient of -1.0 would indicate a perfect, *negative* linear correlation (see Figure 8.5). In this situation, an increase in the value of one variable corresponds precisely to a consistent rate of decrease in the other variable. The relationship between blood-alcohol level and pilot performance is an example of a negative of correlation, where an increase in one variable corresponds to a decrease in the other.

A correlation coefficient of 0.0 would indicate that no relationship exists between the two variables (Spatz & Johnston, 1989). Therefore, the correlation coefficient has the potential to range from −1.0 to +1.0.

It is most unlikely that researchers will obtain a perfect linear correlation when conducting statistical analyses in social science. It is more likely that intermediate correlations will be obtained and the probability level (α) should be used to determine the extent to which the correlation has reached statistical significance. In general, the following list provides a useful guide to the interpretation of correlation coefficients:

Correlation Coefficient	Strength of Relationship
±0.0 to ±0.2	Very Weak
±0.2 to ±0.4	Weak
±0.4 to ±0.7	Moderate
±0.7 to ±0.9	Strong
±0.9 to ±1.0	Very Strong

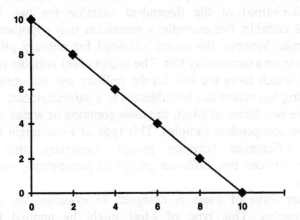

Figure 8.5   An example of a negative linear correlation

In Example 8.1, a research hypothesis was proposed that a relationship would exist between the two variables. Therefore, the null hypothesis proposed that no relationship would exist. The results indicated that the probability that a correlation coefficient of .9902 would have occurred, had the null hypothesis been true, was .001. Since this value is less than .05, the correlation coefficient is said to be statistically significant. Therefore, the null hypothesis can be 'rejected' and the experimental hypothesis is 'supported'.

The most important guideline when interpreting correlation coefficients is that a relationship **does not** necessarily indicate causality. In the case of Example 8.1, the fact that a relationship exists does not necessarily indicate that a lack of flying experience **causes** poor performance in terms of aeronautical knowledge. It merely suggests that a relationship exists between the two variables. While there may be a causal link, it is also possible that an additional variable(s) may be influencing the data, such as inadequate training techniques. In this case, it may not be the fact that pilots lack experience, but that the educational processes may have failed to provide pilots with the necessary skills and knowledge.

8.6.2   t-test

Where a quantitative difference between two groups is hypothesised, and the data meet the criteria for parametric statistical analysis, the *t*-test may be applied. The *t*-test is based upon an analysis of the means and variability (standard deviation) of the dependent variable for two levels of an independent variable. For example, a researcher may hypothesise that there is a difference between the scores obtained for military pilots and non-military pilots on a personality test. The independent variable is the category of pilot, of which there are two levels: military and non-military, and the corresponding test scores can be subjected to a parametric test.

There are two forms of *t*-test, the most common of which is designed to evaluate two independent samples. This type of *t*-test might be applied to determine differences between groups. Generally, this involves a comparison between two different groups of participants, such as experts and novices.

The other form of *t*-test is designed to evaluate two dependent or matched samples. This type of *t*-test might be applied to determine differences within groups (also referred to as repeated measures) such as might occur during a comparison between the pre-training and post-training performance of a single group of participants (before-after design).

Example 8.2 illustrates the application of the independent samples *t*-test applied by Isaac (1994). Isaac (1994) sought to determine whether any differences existed between air traffic controllers and a matched sample of the general population in terms of their scores on the Vividness of Visual Imagery Questionnaire (VVIQ) and the Vividness of Visual Imagery Movement (VMIQ) Questionnaire.

Example 8.2

Mean scores (standard deviations are in parentheses) for the VVIQ and the VMIQ for matched samples of air traffic controllers and the general population (from Isaac, 1994).

	VVIQ		VMIQ	
	$\overline{X}$	*SD*	$\overline{X}$	*SD*
Air Traffic Controllers	63.3	(15.4)	84.9	(33.5)
General Population	92.1	(24)	126.8	(34.9)

The *t*-test is designed to determine the difference between the mean results given the variability of the scores. For example, a greater difference between the means would normally lead to the conclusion that the two groups under examination are derived from different populations. However, this conclusion is dependent upon the extent to which the scores vary. Where there is a large amount of variability within the scores, the result is less conclusive.

The *t*-test calculation can be summarised as the difference between the two means, divided by the standard error of the difference between the means (Robson, 1994). Since the standard error constitutes the standard deviation of the sample means, it enables an assessment of the extent to which the means differ, taking into account their distribution. In most cases, where the difference between the sample means is close to zero, it is more likely that the means were drawn from the same population, and that any differences observed were due to chance.

Equation to Calculate the Independent Samples t-test (t)

$$t = \frac{\overline{X} - \overline{Y}}{\sqrt{\dfrac{\Sigma X^2 - \dfrac{(\Sigma X)^2}{N_x}}{N_x(N_x - 1)} + \dfrac{\Sigma Y^2 - \dfrac{(\Sigma Y)^2}{N_y}}{N_y(N_y - 1)}}}$$

where: X = the score in Group One;
Y = the score in Group Two;
N_x = number of scores in Group One.
N_y = number of scores in Group Two.

$$\sqrt{\frac{\Sigma X^2 - \dfrac{(\Sigma X)^2}{N_x}}{N_x(N_x - 1)} + \frac{\Sigma Y^2 - \dfrac{(\Sigma Y)^2}{N_y}}{N_y(N_y - 1)}} = \text{standard error of the difference between means}$$

Results for Example 8.2

Value of *t*

VVIQ	$t\ (df = 204) = -6.06, p < .0005$
VMIQ	$t\ (df = 204) = -5.18, p < .0005$

Box 8.2

The *t*-test

In our study on the effect of blood alcohol level on pilot performance, we wanted to compare the performance of the three experimental groups and demonstrate that, as hypothesised, the moderate alcohol condition leads to significantly poorer performance than either the low or no alcohol conditions. The *t*-test is one of the most common parametric statistical tests designed for comparing two groups of scores. We referred earlier to the fact that measures of central tendency, such as the mean, provide only a very crude description of a set of data, due to the dispersion of scores.

The *t* test takes into account such a dispersion of scores and, based on these measures, computes values that allow us to conclude whether the sample scores come from the same or different populations. For example, we could compare the high- versus low-alcohol condition; high- versus no alcohol condition; and the low- versus no alcohol condition. Normally, the groups selected for comparison would be guided by the pre-specified experimental hypothesis.

However, it must be noted that where multiple analyses are being conducted on the same data, a correction must be made to the significance level as a means of limiting the probability of a Type I error. This correction can be calculated using a Bonferroni test, in which the significance level is divided by the number of comparisons made between variables. In the case of our study, we intend to make three comparisons and our chosen significance level is .05. Therefore, our corrected level for statistical significance is now .017.

The results arising from Example 8.2 were obtained following comparisons between air traffic controllers and the general population on both the VVIQ and the VMIQ. On the basis of the values for *t*, both sets of results indicate that the differences observed between the means were unlikely to have occurred by chance, given that the null hypothesis was true. Therefore, it can be concluded that the mean results for air traffic controllers and the general population differed significantly on both the VVIQ and VMIQ.

Despite the attraction of the *t* test, it is important to note that there is a limitation to the number of independent comparisons of this kind that can be conducted on a set of data. See the detailed discussion of the principles and computation of the *t*-test in Howell (1997), Minium, King, and Bear (1993), or Kirk (1968), and see Siegel and Castellan (1988) for information pertaining to non-parametric equivalents.

8.6.3 Analysis of Variance

In many cases, researchers will be interested in measuring the differences between not just two, but between three or more groups or variables. The Analysis of Variance (ANOVA) is a useful statistical tool for this more complex kind of comparison.

The ANOVA assesses whether the data arising from a study might belong to the same population, regardless of experimental group, or whether the observations in at least one of the experimental groups might come from a different population. The resulting *F*-statistic is computed by comparing the variability of values within groups with the variability of values between groups (Rowntree, 1991).

If the ANOVA fails to reveal any statistically significant differences between the groups, then there is no purpose in examining the data any further. If the *F*-statistic indicates that there is a difference among the groups, then, guided by the hypotheses and theory, specific comparisons or planned contrasts between pairs of groups can be undertaken to examine where the differences actually lie. More importantly, it is possible to examine whether there is a difference in the expected direction of the difference between means. However, there are limitations to the number of valid, independent contrasts or comparisons that can be undertaken and comparisons should be guided by knowledge of past findings and the theoretical framework on which a study is based.

The experimental design illustrated in Figure 8.6 is an example where an ANOVA could be used to test an experimental hypothesis concerning the relationship between experience and age in diagnosing a particular problem associated with an aircraft engine. It is a two-way design (experience by age) with three levels of each of the between-subjects independent variables. Therefore, the scores could be subjected to a two-way analysis of variance to examine evidence of the two main effects (experience and age) and any interaction between these factors in terms of the time taken to diagnose an engine fault.

Subsequent planned comparisons, motivated by theory, would assess whether differences in performance between the specific conditions are statistically significant. For example, the different levels of experience might be compared to determine whether performance improvements tend to occur with increasing levels of experience.

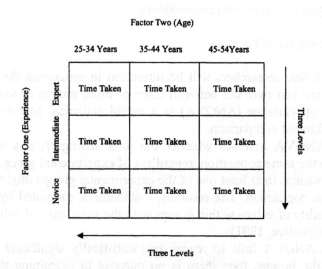

Figure 8.6 An example of an experimental design incorporating two between-subjects factors (experience and age), each of which has three levels

It should be noted that increasing the number of independent variables in an experiment increases both the number of participants required and the complexity of the statistical analysis. Each additional independent variable adds another main effect and increases the number of possible interactions between factors. Therefore, an experiment that consists of three independent variables (A, B, & C) requires a three-way analysis of variance that computes three main effects (A; B; C), three, two-way interactions (A x B; A x C; B x C) and one, three-way interaction (A x B x C).

The interpretation of the meaning of higher-order interactions, such as four-way interactions, becomes increasingly difficult. Consequently, it is recommended that designs include no more than three independent variables. Where the data violate the assumptions of parametric tests, a non-parametric analysis of variance, such as the Friedman analysis of variance by ranks, or a Kruskal-Wallis one way analysis of variance, may be useful (see Siegel & Castellan, 1988).

Box 8.3

Analysis of variance

Consider the two-way design for our study of the effects of blood alcohol on pilot performance. In this case, we also want to consider the impact of age on the results. The experimental design guides our analysis of the data, since it specifies the main effects and interactions that we can examine. Therefore, guided by our theory, we might expect that age will affect performance, and that alcohol will affect performance. These are our two main effects, and they each have a function independent of one another. However, pilot performance may also be influenced by a combination of the two factors such that the performance of older pilots tends to be more affected by the ingestion of alcohol than younger pilots. This constitutes an interaction and is best described using a graph in which the means for each level of each variable are depicted. In the figure below, we see that although the initial performance between the groups appears relatively consistent, the rate of deterioration for older pilots is greatest. Therefore, there is evidence of an interaction between alcohol ingestion and age in terms of pilot performance.

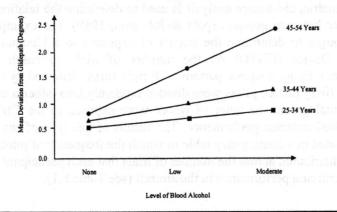

So far, the statistical tests considered relate most directly to data obtained from experimental or quasi-experimental investigations. Where data from rating scales and questionnaires meet the assumptions of parametric tests, they can be analysed using these procedures. However, in some instances, there may be a number of dependent variables being measured. For example, three or four conventional scales or tests may be administered with a view towards measuring the relationship between variables such as anxiety level, accuracy, response latency, personality and experience. In this case, a Multivariate Analysis of Variance (MANOVA) may be the most efficient and effective way to analyse the patterns within and between the different dependent measures (see Tabachnick & Fidell, 1996 for information concerning multivariate statistical procedures).

8.7   Non-Parametric Tests

Non-parametric techniques are adopted when the conditions for the application of parametric statistics are unable to be met, such as a non-normal distribution, a small sample size, or ordinal data. In many cases, each parametric statistic has its own non-parametric equivalent. Some of the more common non-parametric tests include the Chi-Square, Wilcoxon-Mann-Whitney Test, and the Spearman Correlation.

8.7.1   Chi-Square

In situations where the variables are categorical, such as occupations, the non-parametric, chi-square analysis is used to determine the relationships or differences between groups (Spatz & Johnston, 1989). For example, Ortiz (1994) sought to determine the impact of exposure to a Computer-Based Training Device (CBTD) on the number of trials to reach criterion performance flying a square pattern with right turns, followed by 450° turn to North. Sixty novice pilots were divided randomly into either a control or experimental group, the latter of whom were exposed to the CBTD until they reached criterion performance. The results of this type of analysis can be distributed in a contingency table in which the frequency of pilots in each group is distributed across the number of trials that each participant required to reach criterion performance in the aircraft (see Table 8.1).

Table 8.1   Contingency table showing the frequency of pilots in the experimental and control groups distributed across the number of the trials to reach criterion performance (adapted from Ortiz, 1994)

		Number of Trials			
		1	2	3	4
Group	Experimental	16	10	4	0
	Control	1	6	12	11

Where this type of categorical (nominal) data is available, the Chi-square analysis can be used to determine the likelihood of different groups or associations occurring. The Chi-square statistic (χ^2) is based upon an analysis of frequencies, and is specifically designed to compare the frequencies *observed* in each category against those which would have been *expected* to have occurred if there had been no particular relationship between the variables (Spatz & Johnston, 1989). In the case of the data obtained by Ortiz (1994), a difference between the relative frequencies would only be expected if the CBTD had an impact upon performance.

Example 8.3

In this example, the contingency table developed by Ortiz (1994) is used as the basis to demonstrate the application of the Chi-square statistic (see Table 8.1). On the basis of this data, the chi-square can be calculated as follows:

Equation to Calculate the value of Chi-square (χ^2)

$$\chi^2 = \Sigma \frac{(o-e)^2}{e}$$

where: o = the observed frequency;
e = the expected frequency; and
Σ = the sum of the square of the difference between the expected and the observed frequencies, divided by the expected frequency for each of the cells within a contingency table.

The expected frequency (*e*) is calculated on the assumption that no relationship exist between the variables, and that the distribution of frequencies is based upon chance (the null hypothesis). Since it is assumed that each cell is part of one row and one column of the table, the expected value for the cell is calculated as:

$$\text{expected value}(e) = \frac{(\text{row total})(\text{column total})}{\text{grand total}}$$

Results for Example 8.3

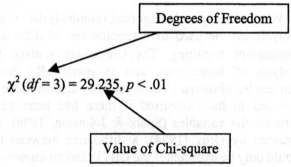

$$\chi^2\,(df = 3) = 29.235, p < .01$$

Since the probability of this value occurring, given that the null hypothesis is true, is less than .01, the null hypothesis can be discarded in favour of the research hypothesis. In the case of Ortiz (1994), the results indicate that a significant difference exists between the expected and the observed frequencies in one or more of the cells of the contingency table.

Although the Chi-square statistic will indicate a difference between the expected and the observed frequencies, the main difficulty is that it does not indicate precisely where this difference lies. Consequently, the researcher must 'inspect' the contingency table to determine the cell/s which were most likely to have contributed to the results observed.

For example, Ortiz (1994) concluded that the difference between the expected and the observed frequencies was most apparent for the control group that reached criterion in one trial, and for the experimental group that reached criterion in four trials. In both cases, the observed frequency was less than the expected frequency.

8.8   Computer Software for Statistical Analysis

A large number of off-the-shelf software packages are available for the computation of basic and more advanced statistical analyses. The use of relatively well-respected packages such as SPSS and StatView, can speed up the process of analysis. However, the most effective user is one who is familiar with the purpose, assumptions, mechanics and calculation of the various statistical tests. Therefore, it is worthwhile to read about common tests such as the *t*-test, ANOVA, and correlation, before embarking on computer-based analyses of a data set. Ultimately, a researcher needs to be able to compute the statistics and be confident that the chosen test is appropriate given the particular set of data, and that the interpretation and reporting of the results is valid and accurate.

8.9   Chapter Summary

Inferential statistics represent some of the most common forms of data analysis that are used in social science research in aviation. They are based upon a common principle of probability of occurrence and the assumption that the results from a random sample can reflect characteristics of the population from which it is drawn. This chapter was designed to introduce the main forms of inferential statistics, including the correlation, *t*-test and the chi-square. It also included a discussion concerning the Type I and Type II errors, as a balance between these two risks has important implications for the conclusions drawn from aviation safety research.

The successful application of inferential statistics is dependent upon the extent to which the data and the methodology meet a number of fundamental assumptions. The distinction was made between parametric and non-parametric forms of inferential data analysis, wherein the latter techniques can be used where the data fail to meet the parametric criteria.

The chapter was designed to provide an introduction to principles of inferential statistics, rather than a step-by-step guide to the implementation of statistical tests in social science. There are number of very useful texts that can provide the researcher with this type of information, some of which are listed in Section 8.10.

8.10   Further Reading

Howell, D.C. (1997). *Statistical methods for psychology* (4th ed.). Belmont, CA: Duxbury Press.

Kachigan, S.K. (1991). *Multivariate statistical analysis: A conceptual introduction.* New York, NY: Radius Press.

Kirk, R.E. (1968). *Experimental design: Procedures for the behavioural sciences.* Belmont, CA: Brooks/Cole.

McGuigan, F.J. (1997). *Experimental psychology: Methods of research* (7th ed.). New Jersey, NJ: Prentice Hall.

Minium, E.W., King, B.M., & Bear, G. (1993). *Statistical reasoning in psychology and education* (3rd ed.). New York, NY: Wiley.

Rowntree, D. (1991). *Statistics without tears: A primer for non-mathematicians.* London, UK: Penguin.

Tabachnick, B.G., & Fidell, L.S. (1996). *Using multivariate statistics* (3rd ed). New York, NY: Harper Collins.

Winer, B.J. (1971). *Statistical principles in experimental design* (2nd ed.). New York, NY: McGraw-Hill.

9 Qualitative Data Analysis

9.1 Introduction

Qualitative data usually take the form of 'words', rather than 'numbers' and have the potential to yield significant information for researchers in terms of the descriptions of events that occur within specified environments (Miles & Huberman, 1994; Strauss & Corbin, 1990). Until relatively recently, the application of qualitative data analysis has been restricted to disciplines such as anthropology and history. This was due to a combination of factors, most significant of which was the view that qualitative analyses lacked the methodological rigor necessary for more scientific endeavours.

Despite this perception, the application of qualitative analyses is more frequent within the social sciences, particularly as techniques for systematically analysing qualitative data become available, and as the differences between quantitative and qualitative analyses become more evident. In particular, quantitative analyses are generally designed to summarise a complex set of data. Inevitably, this process results in the loss of information that might be valuable to the research study.

Qualitative analyses are normally based upon an assumption of *inclusion*, rather than the *exclusion* of data (Brannen, 1992; Coffey & Atkinson, 1996). Consequently, the processes of quantitative and qualitative data analyses are quite different and, although they may appear as substitutes for one another, qualitative and quantitative analyses are most powerful when they are applied as complementary analytical techniques (Brannen, 1992; Henley, 1995).

Miles and Huberman (1994) suggest that the main advantage associated with the application of qualitative data analyses is the capacity to *situate* the data collection and analysis within the real world environment. Consequently, the researcher is immersed within the social or organisational context and acquires data through self-experience as much as through the participants with whom the research may be taking place.

The notion of inclusion as a principle of data acquisition suggests that a more complex but more realistic description of the environment is likely to

159

emerge through qualitative data analysis. This additional information is often referred to as the *richness* of the data, such that it yields more information than what is directly associated with the research question. For example, a researcher may be interested in the perception of safety within a particular carrier, and conducts semi-structured interviews as part of the process of data acquisition. Although the participants may provide a perception of safety, additional information may also arise during data collection, such as 'why the perception exists'. From a quantitative perspective, this additional information may not be necessary for the process of data analysis. However, from a qualitative perspective, the additional data provides an *understanding* of the responses that may have been acquired, and has the capacity to *associate* these responses to a particular operating environment.

One of the main features associated with qualitative data analysis is the capacity to examine complex situations over a *sustained* period (Miles & Huberman, 1994). This provides an opportunity to establish long-term relationships between events and subsequent outcomes. This is typically evident in historical analyses in which the events in one decade or century may impact upon the events within another. In many cases, these changes are not quantifiable. Nevertheless, they reflect a valid and reliable model of the relationship between events.

9.2   Difficulties Associated with Qualitative Data Analysis

By its very nature, qualitative data analysis can be problematic. For example, the process of immersion and self-experience within a domain, and the subsequent reporting of this experience, is susceptible to the researcher's own values and perceptions. Being aware of these perceptions is one thing. However, to actively suppress the inclination is quite another, and it can be difficult to provide an account that is completely free of subjectivity.

The problem of subjectivity can be balanced against a number of issues, including the value of the data that is obtained by virtue of the qualitative analytical process. In many cases, the knowledge that is acquired outweighs any apparent perceptions of subjectivity of the reporting procedure. In addition, there are a number of mechanisms that can be employed to ensure the reliability of the data interpretation, including triangulation and the inclusion of multiple observers where appropriate (Seamster, Redding, & Kaempf, 1997; Miles & Huberman, 1994).

One of the more pragmatic difficulties that tends to arise in qualitative research is the amount of data acquired, and the subsequent management and processing of these data. For example, a ten minute interview at 300 words per minute will yield 3000 words, in addition to any non-verbal cues that may have been apparent. Consequently, the transcription of an hour-long interview across 20 participants can be an arduous task.

Although there are a number of products available to assist with the management of qualitative data, Miles and Huberman (1994) suggest that one of the most important factors to facilitate the efficient acquisition of data requires that a researcher develop a level of familiarity with the environment under examination. Less familiar researchers tend to acquire too much data, and have less capacity to explain and understand the conceptual issues that may arise, and how they relate to the broader domain. One of the solutions may involve the development of a more structured approach initially, which can be modified as the experience of the researcher increases.

9.3 The Process of Qualitative Data Analysis

Consistent with the quantitative approach to data analysis, there are a number of features of the qualitative analytical process that remain consistent, irrespective of the particular type of analysis employed. For example, an over-riding goal associated with qualitative research is to capture, as accurately as possible, the attitudes, perceptions, knowledge and behaviours of individuals within the operational environment (Coffey & Atkinson, 1996). Consistent with this goal, the data acquired through qualitative research are normally retained in their original form throughout the analytical process (Strauss & Corbin, 1990). This preserves both the integrity and the complexity of the information that arises and, therefore, represents a more 'realistic' representation of the data.

The majority of qualitative analytical procedures consist of an analysis of verbal or written information. The main aim is to seek meaning and understanding, and this analytical process can consist of the search for regularities, the search for patterns, the classification of elements, and/or a reconsideration or reflection on existing principles or perceptions (Miles & Huberman, 1994). For example, a researcher may seek responses to a series of open-ended questions and sort these responses into a series of themes.

The range of themes that emerge provides the basis for an understanding of the similarities and differences that may exist within a particular group.

Unlike quantitative research, where the data analysis typically occurs after all the data have been collected, qualitative research involves a process whereby data analysis occurs concurrently with data acquisition. This process involves three main stages (see Figure 9.1) in which the data are reduced to a manageable form, the data are displayed in a manner that facilitates interpretation, and the data are verified for validity and reliability (Bulmer, 1979; Bryman, 1988; Miles & Huberman, 1994).

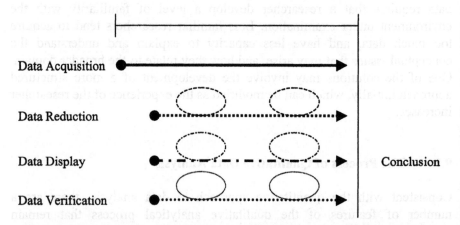

Figure 9.1 An illustration of the qualitative research process in which a series of cyclical strategies occur in parallel

Qualitative data reduction is normally guided by a research question, rather than a hypothesis. The broader nature of research questions enables the investigator to obtain a wide variety of information based upon summaries of field notes or observations, the identification of recurring themes, and/or the classification of information into discrete areas of interest (Pitman & Maxwell, 1992; Strauss & Corbin, 1990).

In most cases, the analysis of qualitative data is driven very much by the nature of the data itself. The researcher is expected to enter into the analytical process with few, if any, preconceived notions about the nature of the data that might be acquired. This strategy ensures that the data are as closely as possible, a direct reflection of the perceptions and behaviours that occur within the environment under examination.

For example, McLean, Palmerton, Chittum, George, and Funkhouser (1998) sought to determine whether sandbags could be employed to simulate passenger behaviour during structural integrity tests of aircraft escape slides. Although it might have been possible to quantify the relationship between the two variables, McLean et al. (1998) elected to employ a qualitative approach in which a description was recorded of the movement of the sandbags as they progressed down the slide.

This was considered the most appropriate form of analysis, since it described a pattern of behaviour in terms that were easily translated into usable information. A test on the suitability of a Boeing 747 slide yielded the following description: 'All bags travelled straight down the slide, but the slide cupped, preventing the [sand] bags from reaching the ground' (McLean et al., 1998, p. 7). This description yields particularly useful information that may not have been readily apparent through a more quantitative approach.

Qualitative information also provides an opportunity to conduct a concurrent interpretation and re-interpretation of the data, such that the outcomes have the capacity to provide more meaningful information (Strauss & Corbin, 1990). In the case of the Boeing 747 slide, it may be useful to note other features associated with the slide, as a way to offer solutions to the problem. Consequently, qualitative data analysis is fluid, and changes can often occur as the analysis progresses.

The displays employed in qualitative data analysis may range from matrices that classify discrete elements, to flow-diagrams or conceptual graphs, that attempt to capture the inter-relationship between elements. Typically, the choice of display will be dependent upon the type of data acquired and the most efficient and effective means to display this type of information.

According to Miles and Huberman (1994), the development of conclusions arising from qualitative data analyses needs to occur in conjunction with the process of verification. This may involve a re-examination of field notes to confirm a particular proposition, or it may involve a detailed discussion and analysis with Subject Matter Experts (SME) and/or colleagues. This process also provides a mechanism for establishing the validity of the information that has been acquired, and the conclusions that have been drawn on the basis of the information.

9.4 Qualitative Techniques in Aviation

Qualitative data may emerge from a number of non-experimental research strategies including secondary records, field observations, task analyses, case studies, critical incidents, or surveys/interviews. However, due to the nature of qualitative research, there are also a number of strategies available to examine the data including the thematic approach, concept (cognitive) mapping, process tracing, protocol analysis, cognitive interview, and conceptual graph analysis. One or more of these strategies may be applied, depending upon the characteristics associated with the data. There are a number of additional strategies that might be applied, but which are beyond the scope of this text. More information can be obtained from a text that specialises in qualitative data analytical techniques (see Section 9.12).

Qualitative research techniques are typically applied in situations where little is known about a particular domain, and/or the level of data required extends beyond that available through quantitative analytical techniques. Within the aviation environment, qualitative data analyses have been applied in a number of research domains including system safety (Ratner & Guselli, 1995), accident investigation (Helmreich, 1994), flight instruction (Henley, 1991; 1995), and naturalistic decision-making (Klein, 1990; Urban, Weaver, Bowers, & Rhodenizer, 1996).

9.5 Thematic Approach

The thematic approach to qualitative data analysis involves the development of factors or themes that underlie the information obtained from participants. For example, a series of interviews with experienced air traffic controllers may yield statements that, on the surface appear quite distinct. However, by searching for patterns in the transcripts of interviews, it may be possible to establish links between perceptions or statements and, thereby, develop a theme (Coffey & Atkinson, 1996).

The thematic approach is particularly useful with large amounts of data as it represents both a process of data analysis and a process of data reduction. Moreover, the identification of themes provides a level of reliability for the responses made by individuals. In other words, it may appear to be a perception that holds true across the participants within a domain.

Miles and Huberman (1994) suggest that underlying themes will, more or less, emerge throughout the process of qualitative data acquisition. This is consistent with the experience encountered by Henley (1995), following a series of semi-structured interviews with flight instructors in both Canada and Australia.

According to Henley (1995), it was possible to classify responses on the basis of themes, clusters and related questions. Moreover, this process occurred in a cyclical strategy as information was acquired. Henley (1995) developed a mechanism to code and index the information to facilitate the process of data reduction and interpretation.

The use of coding is designed to enable the development of an understanding of the central features that underpin the perceptions and behaviours of a particular social/occupational group or environment (Coffey & Atkinson, 1996; Miles & Huberman, 1994). This structured search for a series of central theoretical features is often referred to as *grounded theory*, and it represents an important approach to qualitative research (Brannen, 1992; Strauss, 1987).

However, it should be noted that one of the difficulties associated with the application of coding mechanisms is that it may restrict the complexity and the variety of information that can be considered (P. Woods, 1985). Henley (1995) overcomes this problem by considering separately, any information that lies outside the coding structure. Moreover, both Peshkin (1993) and Henley (1995) caution that the features that comprise the coding structure should be organised around the data, rather than organising the data around the coding structure as might be the case in a more quantitative approach.

9.6   Concept Mapping

Like the thematic approach, concept mapping is also employed as a means of establishing grounded theoretical perspectives. It generally involves a small number of participants who construct a diagrammatic representation of the relationship between task-related components and associated conceptual bases of performance (Sowa, 1990). Typically, the conceptual map undergoes a series of structured iterations as the domain is further defined and explored in consultation with the participants involved.

The data are depicted as a schematic diagram in which nodes are linked by directional arrows. According to Thordsen (1991), the directional links can also include information pertaining to the characteristics of the link (see Figure 9.2). However, it should be noted that this type of analytical process is generally associated with a specific task, rather than with the more global descriptions that are associated with other forms of qualitative data analysis.

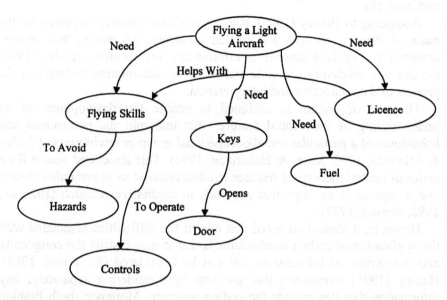

Figure 9.2 An example of a concept map for flying a light aircraft (adapted from Thordsen, 1991)

The major advantage associated with this approach is that a reasonably reliable model can be developed through a progression of interactions with relatively few participants. Moreover, it represents another means by which data can be limited to a (relatively) manageable level (Rasmussen, 1990). However, the primary disadvantage associated with conceptual mapping is the potential reliance upon a relatively small number of participants. This may limit the extent to which the principles identified can be generalised across the domain under examination.

9.7   Process Tracing Methods

Where concept mapping relies intrinsically upon participants to recall the cognitive elements associated with a particular domain, process tracing is a technique whereby the cognitive elements are inferred from the behaviour of decision-makers. In particular, inferences are made on the basis of the sequence and type of information acquired. For example, Wiggins and Henley (1997) considered the sequence in which information was accessed during a computer-based decision-making exercise involving experienced and inexperienced instructors. A process tracing map was constructed for each participant, and the similarities and differences were used as the basis for inferences concerning the decision-making process employed (see Figure 9.3).

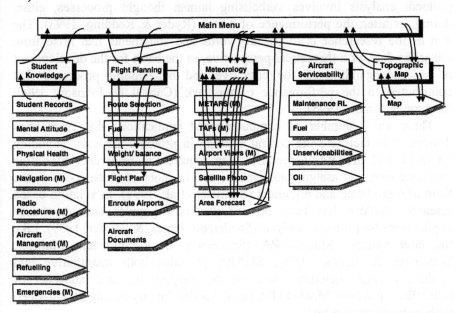

Figure 9.3   An example of a process tracing map for computer-based flight instructor decision-making (Wiggins & Henley, 1997)

In general, process tracing has been used in aviation as one means of differentiating expert from novice performance (Kirschenbaum, 1992; Wiggins & O'Hare, 1995; Wiggins & Henley, 1997). However, the main disadvantage associated with the approach is that, while it is useful as a means of differentiating performance, it does not necessarily explain or identify the causes of the differentiation. Consequently, process tracing is typically used in conjunction with other forms of qualitative data analysis such as protocol analysis.

9.8   Protocol Analysis

Protocol analysis has been used extensively in aviation and allied domains as a means of acquiring knowledge associated with the cognitive performance of individuals during the performance of complex tasks (Ball, Evans, & Dennis, 1994; Bowers, Deaton, Oser, Prince, & Kolb, 1995; Hess, 1987; Koubek, Salvendy, & Noland, 1994; Lee, 1991). Specifically, protocol analysis involves verbalising human thought processes, either during, or after, the performance of a task (Ryder & Redding, 1993). The aim of the researcher is to use keywords and statements that arise from either the data, or a theoretical perspective, as the basis for the development of an understanding of the cognitive and behavioural processes that contributed to the performance of the task (Carroll & Johnson, 1990; Ericsson & Simon, 1996).

There are a number of computer-based applications that have been developed to facilitate the coding strategy in protocol analysis, including NUDIST and SHAPA. Generally, they require the researcher to define various codes, and assign statements to one or more of these codes in the form of a predicate and argument (Seamster et al., 1997). In aviation-based research, SHAPA has been one of the most popular computer-based applications for protocol analysis (Sanderson, James, & Seidler, 1989). Like the later version, MacSHAPA (Sanderson, Scott, Johnston, Mainzer, Watanabe, & James, 1994), SHAPA provides both quantitative and qualitative data including flow charts, frequencies, and analyses of reliability. However, MacSHAPA has the added facility of integrating video with audio or written text.

Although protocol analysis has been used extensively as a research tool, the efficacy of this approach is reliant upon the capacity of the task to elicit the key cognitive processes involved. Moreover, a number of authors have referred to the unreliability of participants in accurately describing the nature of the cognitive processes involved in the performance of a task (Carroll & Johnson, 1990; Nisbett & Wilson, 1977). This is particularly evident during retrospective verbal protocol analyses where there may be a tendency to 'justify' a particular strategy or decision (Cooke, 1994; Hoffman, 1987; Nisbett & Wilson, 1977).

While a verbal protocol concurrent with an experimental task has the advantage of minimising the probability of justification, there is evidence to suggest that the process of thinking-aloud may detract, to some extent, from the performance of the original task (Ericsson & Simon, 1996). Moreover, concurrent protocols are not necessarily able to capture the 'unconscious' processes that may impact upon behaviour in complex, dynamic environments. Nevertheless, a protocol may embody a number of 'indicators' of underlying cognitive activity such as a reference to a previous experience, or an assumption based upon prior knowledge. However, in each case, the identification of underlying cognitive structures may require a level of interpretation on the part of the researcher.

Although there is little doubt that the data arising from verbal protocol analyses should be interpreted with some caution, the variability inherent within the data may be minimised, to some extent, through the development of clear and concise theoretical guidelines (Svenson, 1989). In addition, the procedure needs to facilitate the application of probe questions, if and when the information arising from the participant is insufficient to explain the cognitive strategies involved. This is consistent with the procedure involved in a semi-structured interview technique, and is designed to provide a framework within which to both limit the amount of data required, and maintain a high level of reliability and validity.

9.9   Conceptual Graph Analysis

Conceptual Graph Analysis (CGA) is a technique wherein the data arising from qualitative research techniques can be modelled and integrated into a diagrammatic structure using a series of rules and guidelines (Gordon, Schmierer, & Gill, 1993). This approach differentiates CGA from the more fluid approach associated with conceptual mapping, and is designed to provide a level of reliability for the development of diagrammatic models of human performance.

Consistent with other analytical approaches in aviation, CGA is generally associated with the performance of a relatively specific task. In particular, it focuses upon the cognitive elements of task performance such as perceptions, knowledge and attitudes of participants. Gordon et al. (1993)

refer to these cognitive elements as nodes, and these are linked according to a series of rules that define their relationship (see Figure 9.4).

There are two categories of node: concepts and statements. The information within conceptual nodes is similar to declarative (factual) knowledge, and defines that knowledge of a concept that is required to initiate and/or respond to a particular statement. For example, a successful response to a deterioration in weather conditions in-flight is dependent upon an understanding of cloud types and the implications of concepts such as visibility and cloud-base. Knowledge of these concepts facilitates the recognition of the situation, and enables an appropriate response to be generated.

Conceptual nodes are typically depicted hierarchically, with the overall concept at the head of the diagram. These concepts are linked directly to statement nodes, the information within which can loosely be equated to the notion of procedural or action-oriented knowledge. Unlike conceptual nodes, statement nodes are divided into one of five categories: goals, goal/action statements, style, events and states (Gordon et al. 1993).

Goal nodes designate desired outcomes, and generally direct the nature and structure of subordinate goals, events and states. According to Gordon et al. (1993), state nodes represent features associated with the operating environment that remain consistent across a particular event. When changes occur, nodes represent this change across either a time frame or in response to an event occurring within the environment. For example, an event is triggered when an aircraft reaches its top of descent prior to landing. Where there is a particular reference to the type of change that occurred, a style node is used to describe the precise nature of the change. For example, it may be necessary to specify the rate of descent of an aircraft rather than simply that a descent occurred.

Although the CGA has the advantage of a relatively prescribed format in which to represent data, it suffers the disadvantage of a lack of flexibility that might be desired in some forms of qualitative research. However, it should be recalled that CGA represents one of a number of means of representing the data arising from qualitative research. Therefore, its application will depend upon the nature of the domain, the data acquired, and the aims and objectives of the researcher.

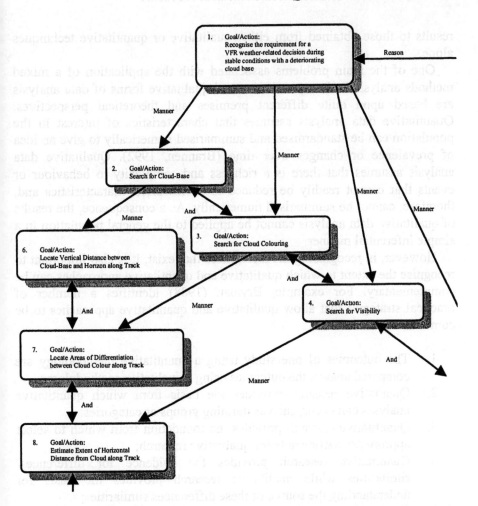

Figure 9.4 An example of part of a conceptual graph developed according to CGA principles and guidelines

9.10 Mixed Methods Data Analysis

Given the difficulties associated with both quantitative and qualitative analytical techniques, there is a strong movement towards the application of a combination of strategies incorporating both qualitative and quantitative forms of data analysis. This type of strategy is referred to as *mixed methods* analysis, and Bryman (1992) argues that it has the capacity to yield superior results to those obtained from either qualitative or quantitative techniques alone.

One of the main problems associated with the application of a mixed methods analysis is that quantitative and qualitative forms of data analysis are based upon quite different premises and theoretical perspectives. Quantitative data analysis assumes that characteristics of interest in the population can be standardised and summarised numerically to give an idea of prevalence or changes over time (Brannen, 1992). Qualitative data analysis assumes that there is a richness and complexity to behaviour or events that cannot readily be reduced to standardised characteristics and, therefore, cannot be summarised numerically. As a consequence, the results of qualitative data analysis cannot be applied to the general population in a simple inferential manner.

However, in recognising the differences that exist, it is also important to recognise the extent to which qualitative and quantitative approaches can be complementary. For example, Bryman (1988) identifies a number of practical strategies that allow qualitative and quantitative approaches to be combined:

1. The outcomes of one study using a quantitative methodology are compared against the outcomes using a qualitative methodology;
2. Qualitative research provides the basis from which quantitative analyses can occur, such as defining groups or categories;
3. Quantitative research provides the foundation from which to select appropriate participants for qualitative research;
4. Quantitative research provides the evidence for differences/ similarities while qualitative research provides the basis for understanding the source of these differences/similarities;
5. Quantitative research is used to provide the researcher's perspective, while qualitative research provides the basis for understanding the perspective of the participant;
6. Quantitative research facilitates the generalisation of the results arising from qualitative research; and
7. Qualitative research is applied within quasi-experimental research (adapted from Bryman, 1998).

Within the aviation environment, mixed methods analyses have been limited to a small number of domains including flight instruction (Henley, 1995), decision-making (Klein et al., 1989), and error management (Dutke,

1994). However, Henley (1995) suggests that the mixed methods approach has the capacity to provide a great deal of additional information concerning the complexity of the inter-relationships that occur within the aviation environment.

9.11   Chapter Summary

This chapter described a number of qualitative strategies for data analysis that might be applied either in conjunction with, or as alternatives to, quantitative strategies. These strategies included the thematic approach, concept mapping, process tracing, protocol analysis, and conceptual graph analysis. Each has advantages and disadvantages depending upon the type of research and the nature of the methodology. However, the aim was to provide an overview of the various options available to the researcher to acquire and process qualitative data within the aviation environment.

The chapter concluded with an outline of the mixed-methods approach to data acquisition and analysis in which both qualitative and quantitative strategies are employed to provide a complementary response to a research question or hypothesis.

9.12   Further Reading

Brannen, J. (1992). Combining qualitative and quantitative approaches: An overview. In J. Brannen (Ed.), *Mixing methods: Qualitative and quantitative research.* Aldershot, UK: Ashgate.

Bryman, A. (1988). *Quantity and quality in social research.* London, UK: Unwin Hyman.

Coffey, A., & Atkinson, P. (1996). *Making sense of qualitative data.* Thousand Oaks, CA: Sage.

Cohen, L., & Manion, L. (1986). *Research methods in education* (2nd ed.). London, UK: Croom Helm.

Ericsson, K.A., & Simon, H.A. (1996). *Protocol analysis: verbal reports as data.* Cambridge, MA: MIT Press.

Miles, M.B., & Huberman, A.M. (1994). *Qualitative data analysis* (2nd ed.). Thousand Oaks, CA: Sage.

Strauss, A. (1987). *Qualitative analysis for social scientists.* Cambridge, UK: Cambridge University Press.

Strauss, A., & Corbin, J. (1990). *Basics of qualitative research.* Newbury Park, CA: Sage.

10 Publishing Research

10.1 Introduction

Having conducted a long and possibly labour-intensive study, researchers have an obligation both to publish this information as a means of adding to the existing knowledge base, and to communicate the information to participating organisations. There are a number of ways in which the research might be published, and the choice will be dependent upon the nature of the study and the audience to whom the research is directed.

This chapter describes some of the mechanisms available to publish the results arising from social science research within aviation. These include refereed journals, electronic journals, conference papers, and unrefereed journals. Given the nature of social science research in aviation, it may be necessary to consider more than one publication in order to ensure that the research outcomes are available both to members of the academic community and to members of the aviation industry.

For each type of publication, this chapter considers the format and structure in detail, as well as some of the practical issues in submitting a work for publication.

Issues of authorship are considered, drawing attention to the significance of recognising the contribution of others to the overall research outcomes. Furthermore, it is extremely important to safeguard the identity of participants in the study, and ensure that there is no case for plagiarism, either intentional or unintentional.

The chapter concludes with a discussion of the role of magazine articles as the means for disseminating research findings within the aviation industry. In particular, the style of writing is considered, since it differs significantly from that required for refereed journals and conference publications.

10.2 Publishing Research Reports

Research reports are the primary means through which the outcomes of research are communicated to other researchers and practitioners. This communication process may take a number of forms, from an academic journal, through to an article in a local magazine. The aim is to ensure that the outcomes of the research process are disseminated as widely as possible, both for comment and for the information of the readership.

From an academic perspective, publications are normally divided into two categories: refereed and unrefereed. The notion of a refereed publication implies that it will be subjected to an independent review by a panel of experts, prior to being accepted for publication. Most academic journals and some conference submissions are examples of refereed publications. However, it should be noted that the process of review is such that it can take a considerable amount of time before a refereed article is published.

Unrefereed publications generally take the form of a magazine article, where an editor, who may or may not be familiar with a particular area of study, conducts the review. In most instances, the decision to publish a magazine article will be based more on the perceived interest to the readership than the quality of the research methodology and outcomes.

10.3 Ethical Issues and Publication

Irrespective of the type of publication, it is important to consider the ethical issues involved in the dissemination of material. In particular, the anonymity of participants must be safeguarded. Reference to a 'large national and international air carrier in New Zealand' leaves the reader with little option but to conclude that the participants were drawn from Air New Zealand. As a result, the anonymity of both the participants and the organisation may have been violated. Generally speaking, authors should de-identify participants as much as possible, while maintaining sufficient information to facilitate the replication of the study.

A secondary, though no less important, issue regarding publication concerns 'authorship'. Typically, research findings are the product of collaboration between individual professionals or student colleagues, between members of different organisations, or between a supervisor and a student. The question of authorship on subsequent conference, journal or book publications is important and, as it is a potentially sensitive issue, it may deserve consideration at the beginning, rather than at the end of the research process. For example, it is important to discuss the relative contribution expected of chief and associate investigators. The time commitment of members of the research team should also be identified in terms of the conceptual and/or practical aspects of the project. Normally, authorship requires that a person be involved in either the formulation of the research problem, the design of the study, the conduct and interpretation of statistical analyses, and/or the composition of the manuscript. Data collection, data entry, and the provision of financial support for the project do not necessarily qualify for authorship, although the contribution of others should be acknowledged in the Author note that is included as part of the paper.

Where a researcher is given access to data collected and owned by another researcher or group of researchers, authorship must be mutually agreed upon before the commencement of data analysis. Other rules of thumb include assigning authorship to persons only for work they have actually performed or to which they have contributed and, in instances where an article is substantially based on a student's dissertation or thesis, the student would usually be listed as the principal author.

10.4   Publishing in Refereed Journals

The research process commences with a thorough search and review of the literature relating to a particular research question. Once data collection, analysis and interpretation are complete, it is important for a research project to add to the existing body of knowledge. In particular, the publication of findings allows others to benefit from the expected (or unexpected) findings, and to develop an understanding of innovative techniques and interpretations. More generally, the publication of a study may contribute to the advancement of the field.

The task of writing a scientific journal article is both challenging and rewarding. While it represents an opportunity to explain research outcomes, it also represents an opportunity to clarify ideas and concepts within a highly organised structure.

Publishing within a refereed journal also allows the study to be reviewed by qualified researchers, each of whom has experience within the field. Although this process of review is an important part of the academic endeavour, the main objective is to allow a piece of scholarly work to be examined in detail, to ensure that the published paper has a suitable level of rigour and credibility. Consequently, researchers must be prepared to accept the criticism that may emerge, and consider the comments as constructive.

10.5   Selecting an Appropriate Journal

The first task in preparing a research paper for publication in a refereed journal, even before writing the article, is to select a journal in which to have the article published. This decision requires a small amount of research and is crucial if the project is to succeed, as the way in which the article is constructed and presented is related intimately to the focus and readership of the destination journal. In fact, some of the most established researchers are likely to have a target journal in mind for the eventual publication of research that they are about to commence. In essence, it is important to locate a journal that maximises the coverage and impact of the research findings.

One of the most effective ways to select an appropriate journal is to ask a number of questions of the study and identify the intention behind its publication. A small number of the key international journals should be identified within a specialist field. These should be analysed in terms of the focus and format of the articles. In particular, it is important to consider:

1. Which journal is most often the source of articles used in the design of the present study? For example, a large number of references may come from a particular journal and, therefore, it may be the most appropriate outlet for the research outcomes;

2. Who are the members of the editorial board and is their work cited in the study being submitted for publication? Again, it is important to consider the degree to which the journal publishes research within a particular area, and whether the editors (and possible reviewers) are likely to be sympathetic to particular perspectives and paradigms;

3. How many experiments or studies are reported in the sample articles? Some journals require the inclusion of a number of studies or experiments; and

4. Read the *Instructions to Authors* inside the front or back cover of a recent issue of the journal. It is important to note the focus area and theme of the journal, and whether the readership and the target audience are appropriate.

In many cases, the selection of a journal will also be dependent upon more practical issues, such as the rate of rejection and the length of publication waiting lists. Some prestigious journals have very high rates of rejection, although the feedback from the reviewers may be quite helpful for future publications. These journals may also have long waiting lists for publication, and the time involved needs to be weighed against the need for the material to be published as quickly as possible.

Another issue that may need to be considered is the language in which a journal is published. Researchers, for whom English is not their first language, may be more comfortable publishing in their first language, particularly during the initial stages of their career. However, the difficulty associated with this strategy is that these journals may be less widely read and there may be relatively less exposure of the work to the scientific community.

Once a target journal has been selected, the planning and design of the manuscript can begin. It is important to keep in mind the journal readership and the structure of the article to ensure that it conforms to the *Instructions to Authors* guidelines.

10.6   Planning the Manuscript

Ascertain the word limit for articles in the destination journal. Word length will vary across journals, but a maximum of 4,500 words is likely to be a good limit to set. Some journals also include shorter articles (approximately 2,000 words) under a Notes and Commentary, or Practitioner section, and this may be an appropriate outlet to report a small-scale study.

It is important to set a deadline for the completion of the manuscript. With the data collection and analysis complete, the actual writing of the paper can take more time than might be expected. If the work was presented as part of a thesis, there may be a need to update some references and ensure that the theoretical material being used in the introductory section is as up-to-date as possible.

The presentation of the research at a local conference can act as an effective deadline for the development of a manuscript. Although the conference presentation is likely to be oral, it is both useful and impressive to distribute copies of the paper on which the presentation is based. The paper can be a draft of the proposed journal article, and the distribution of the paper allows the dissemination of a much more detailed account of the study than can be conveyed in a brief, oral presentation. More importantly, it may attract some useful feedback and suggestions from specialists, colleagues, and even potential journal reviewers in the area.

10.7 Developing the Structure of the Manuscript

Just as with any lengthy written document, such as a position paper, report or thesis, the journal manuscript requires careful planning. It should be noted that the article is being written for a particular audience and the paper should be framed accordingly. One of the most important features that a reviewer will look for is the readability and accessibility of the article. The study, as interesting or as complex as it is, must be packaged so that it is digested easily, and written with a clarity and attention to detail that permits replication and prevents misinterpretation. Therefore, prospective authors should study other journal articles and analyse their structure and organisation of ideas, the way in which a particular perspective is conveyed and defended, the succinct presentation of methodological detail, and the levels of analysis and interpretation in the discussion section.

Planning the sequence of the article can be achieved in different ways. A flowchart may be a useful aid in this process. The topic sentence can be specified for each paragraph to ensure that there is a logical flow and development of ideas from beginning to end. Some researchers find using small record cards to be useful. These can detail the various points of the study and can be organised and reorganised in a variety of ways.

Realistically, with a word limit of around 4,500 words, there are not many degrees of freedom. For example, an experimental paper falls naturally into the broad sections, Introduction, Method, Results, Discussion, Conclusion. Within the limits of the word count, the format will be something like: Introduction (2,200 words); Method (400 words); Results (600 words); and Discussion (1,300 words).

There are a number of useful sources of information on writing journal articles. The *Publication Manual of the American Psychological Association*

(American Psychological Association, 1994) is an excellent guide. In addition to providing information on the clear expression of ideas through style and grammar, the Manual lists guidelines for nonsexist language, avoiding ethnic bias, and details of editorial style.

10.8 Drafting and Re-drafting the Manuscript

Manuscripts for publication go through many drafts and revisions. A draft should be prepared and then redrafted until it approximates the intended finished product. It is important for authors to obtain feedback on the clarity and accuracy of the paper. Copies of the manuscript may be distributed to colleagues and their comments sought. It can also be useful to seek assistance from colleagues from outside a research area to read the manuscript and assess the degree to which it can be comprehended easily. The formation of publication syndicates may be a helpful aid to this process.

In essence, the publication syndicate comprises research or work colleagues who distribute their manuscripts to one another and come together to discuss structural, editorial, methodological and conceptual issues. This process is most effective where the manuscript is distributed and then discussed after each member has read and annotated the paper.

10.9 Turning a Research Thesis into a Journal Article

The word length for a research Masters or Doctoral thesis permits the inclusion of considerable conceptual and methodological detail, and the luxury of discussing a wide range of ideas. However, in converting a thesis into a journal article, there needs to be significant surrendering of some of this detail. In fact, some of the most cherished aspects of a study may need to be omitted from a shorter, linear journal article. It is possible, of course, to simply cut and paste sections of the thesis to create a smaller document. However, reviewers are familiar with this technique and articles composed in this way often lack coherence and a clear flow of ideas.

When producing an article from a thesis, there is a requirement to reshape and rewrite sections, such that the material flows and a sound, cogent argument unfolds. The *Association for Support of Graduate Students* presents some useful information on techniques for publishing theses (http://www.asgs.org/).

10.10 Formatting the Manuscript

Manuscripts submitted for publication in refereed journals should normally be typed with double spacing throughout, including references, tables, and figure captions. Margins of 2-4 cm should be left on all sides and the pages should be numbered consecutively. Page 1 should include the title of the article and a running header of not more than 40 characters, including spaces. The specific *Instructions to Authors* should be checked for whether names and contact details of the authors are to be included on the title page. In many instances, papers are sent out for 'blind' review, so that author names appear only in the covering letter to the editor of the journal.

Page 2 should include an abstract of 100-150 words (again, it is important to check the specific requirements of the target journal). The abstract is one of the most significant structural elements of the journal article. It is a self-contained summary of the paper that includes a brief account of the research problem, the methodology, results and some of the main conclusions. The main role of the abstract is to assist the reader to determine whether or not the paper is of interest. Therefore, it must be very clear and concise, and must accurately describe the nature of the study. The order of subsequent sections is text, references, tables, figure captions, and figures, each of which begins on a separate page.

Depending upon the style, footnotes should be avoided. Essential footnotes are indicated by superscript figures in the text and appear in a separate section at the end of the manuscript, preceding the references. Appropriate headings and subheadings should be used to indicate the organisation of the paper.

Tables and figures should be numbered consecutively with Arabic numerals in order of appearance within the text. The appropriate place in the article where the table or figure is to be inserted should be indicated using the following format:

**************************'
Figure 1 about here
****

Figures should be submitted camera-ready, and the figures and lettering should be drawn so as to be legible after a reduction of 50 percent.

Author notes can also be included, and should be prepared on a separate page. The information contained in the Notes section may include an acknowledgement of funding or support from organisations or academic institutions, or acknowledgements of trademarks cited in the article (e.g. software used for the design of an experiment). Acknowledgements of contributions and assistance from colleagues, publication syndicate members, reviewers, and research assistants should also be noted in this section. Contact details for reprints of the article or access to stimuli or custom software can also be included. Contact details are particularly important where an article has multiple authors who may be located at different institutions.

10.11 Presentation of Results

An important aspect of research is the ability to convey information about the study and results to an audience either in the form of a report, journal article, book chapter, or conference presentation. Regardless of the medium, an accurate, simple, and communicative format is essential. Most texts on research methods provide detailed accounts of appropriate ways to present data (e.g. Rowntree, 1991; Solso & Johnson, 1984). The key points in presenting the results are to:

- Summarise and collate the raw data in such a way that the audience can glean the necessary patterns and information quickly and accurately;
- Use a diagram, usually a graph, that gives a picture of the quantities involved;
- Use a suitable figure to indicate central tendency and the dispersion of scores.

Crucially, the type of table, diagram or figure that is used will depend on whether the data refer to category variables or to quantity variables. For example, if a researcher wishes to illustrate the frequency with which different categories were mentioned by respondents in a survey on methods of transport used to travel to work (bicycle, car, bus, train, etc), the data could be presented in the form of a frequency table. The table might include the method of transport in one column, the percentage of workers using that method in the second column and the actual number in the sample in the final column (see Rowntree, 1991, p. 39). Alternatively, a block diagram or bar chart could be used wherein the height of the block is proportional to the number of workers in the category. Finally, a pie chart might be an effective way to illustrate the pattern of responses, with the size of the segment being proportional to the frequency of each category. Rowntree (1991) suggests that the pie chart is most effective for a comparison between a category and the total, whereas the block diagram seems clearer if the comparison is to emphasise a comparison between one category and another.

Quantity variables such as heart rate or reaction time can be represented as a frequency distribution. However, as these variables are continuous, rather than discrete categories, it is appropriate to represent the grouped frequencies as a histogram. In a frequency histogram, like the block diagram, the height of the column is proportional to the frequency of response. The difference is that the continuity of the independent variable is reflected in the continuing numerical values shown on the horizontal axis. Where the quantity gradations on the horizontal axis are fine enough, it may be appropriate to present the data in the form of a line graph.

10.11.1 Computer Software for Graphing Data

Many statistical, spreadsheet, and graphing software packages provide the means for fast and pleasing graphical representations of data including Cricket Graph, Excel, SPSS, StatView, and MatLab. It is important to ensure that the figure format is appropriate for the data and that the scale used by the computer gives an accurate reflection of scores, differences, and patterns of dispersion.

10.12 Referencing

Unless otherwise specified, references should be arranged alphabetically according to the names of the authors. Write journal names in full. The *Instructions for Authors* for each journal will specify the referencing requirements. The Publication Manual of the American Psychological Association (American Psychological Association, 1994) or the Chicago Manual of Style (University of Chicago, 1993) are likely to be good starts. The World-Wide Web can also be useful for tracking down particular referencing styles. With the increase in electronic journals and the accessibility to articles found on the Web, it is also important to be able to cite this material accurately.

The most common technique for citing an article from an e-journal is:

Latimer, C., & Stevens, C. (1997). Some remarks on wholes, parts and their perception. *Psycoloquy* *8(13)* Part Whole Perception (1). http://www.cogsci.soton.ac.uk/cgi/psyc /newpsy?

10.13 Submitting the Manuscript

Once a manuscript is complete, the paper can be submitted to the editor of the journal. Typically, multiple copies need to be posted. The *Instructions for Authors* in a recent issue of the journal will detail the number of copies and the full name and address of the editor to whom the manuscript should be sent. A correctly formatted floppy disk with a copy of the manuscript may also need to be included.

The covering letter should be addressed to the editor of the journal, and the authors and the title of the paper should be stated clearly. Include the full contact details of one of the authors including name; postal address; phone number; fax number; and e-mail address. Normally, journal editors will require that the covering letter be signed by all authors.

10.14 The Publication Process

Having sent the manuscript to a journal there are a number of stages before the article appears in print. The first stage in the publication process is receipt of the manuscript by the editor. An acknowledgement of the manuscript being received and a reference number for future correspondence is usually despatched within a few weeks. Depending on the size and scope of the journal, the editor may act as the point of contact or the manuscript may be directed to a subeditor who will oversee the review and feedback process. The manuscript is then distributed to reviewers.

Reviewers are specialists in the field who are asked to read the manuscript and comment on its suitability for publication. The editor receives feedback from the reviewers, collates the responses, and advises the author on whether the paper is to be accepted, resubmitted after minor or major revisions, or rejected. Each reviewer makes a recommendation to the editor but, in most cases, it is the responsibility of the editor to make the final decision on the status of the paper.

There are four possibilities following the submission of a manuscript: i) acceptance of the manuscript for publication as is; ii) acceptance for publication subject to the completion of specified minor revisions; iii) a request for a major revision of the manuscript according to the points raised by the reviewers and the resubmission of the manuscript for a second review; iv) rejection of the manuscript. It is possible for a manuscript to go through a couple of versions before a final copy is accepted for inclusion in the next available volume. Proofs of the typeset article are generally sent to authors prior to publication, and these require prompt but careful proofreading and checking. An author may also request additional reprints of the journal article from the publisher at this time.

10.15 Publishing as a Conference Paper

Details of conferences can be found in specialist journals, newsletters of professional societies and associations, and the World-Wide Web. They represent a useful strategy to publish an article in an environment that is less rigorous than a refereed journal.

Generally, articles for conferences are solicited through a *Call for Papers*. This process may involve the distribution of pamphlets and/or advertisements in relevant journals. Presenters are usually asked to submit an abstract for consideration, rather than an entire paper (there are exceptions). In addition, there is often a level of flexibility in terms of the types of papers that may be presented. For example, some conferences include both research studies, and position papers, while others might also include practitioner papers. The main aim is to allow a certain level of flexibility in terms of the dissemination of information.

Most conferences will require that a paper be submitted for the proceedings of the conference. However, the precise format will depend upon the discipline and the nature of the publication. For example, both the European Association for Aviation Psychology and the Australian Aviation Psychology Association conferences publish proceedings as authored books. Consequently, there are strict publication guidelines that need to be adhered to if the work is to be published.

In general, research reports can be written using the standard format: Introduction, Methodology, Results, Discussion and References. Position papers may require a different structure, although it should be noted that conference papers are usually restricted to a relatively small number of pages in comparison to refereed journals. Therefore, authors need to create a balance between the amount of information provided and the pragmatic requirements of space.

Good presentation technique demands that presenters have the written article available for distribution at the conference. This allows other researchers to refer to the work, prior to the distribution of proceedings, and provides an opportunity to obtain more detailed responses than might be obtained through the presentation of the work alone. In addition, presenters need to take great care when presenting the work, to ensure that the information is clearly understood and is presented within time limits. Normally, presentations are limited to 20 minutes with 10 minutes available for questions.

An important part of the conference publication involves the delivery. In some cases, researchers may elect to submit a *poster presentation* in which a short summary of research outcomes is presented, usually in the form of a display. This strategy has an advantage where researchers may be unsure of their presentation skills, and/or the research involves preliminary data. However, the poster presentation also allows more discussion than might be afforded by an oral presentation, since there are usually no time limits involved.

When developing poster presentations, it is important to ensure that the information is presented in a concise and appealing format. Usually, a 22-point font size is necessary to facilitate readability from a distance. Graphic illustrations are also very useful for poster presentations as they enable a greater amount of information to be acquired in a relatively short period of time. Although the poster only allows for a limited amount of information to be displayed, a summary paper can be distributed that includes a more detailed description of the study.

Oral conference presentations are very much dependent upon the skills of the presenter. Inexperienced presenters, in particular, should be as familiar with the paper as possible, and ensure that visual aids are clear, appealing and reliable. Where oral presentations are concerned, simplicity is usually the best policy. Presentations involving a number of modes of delivery are often faced with problems, particularly in terms of the reliance on technology.

Overhead projection slides are the most common form of visual aid used in oral conference presentations. They can be very effective in communicating information and providing an aide-mémoire for the presenter. In general, the information displayed on an overhead projection slide should be limited to key points that are then expounded by the presenter. As a rule of thumb, text on an overhead slide should be limited to no more than 15 words. The use of graphic illustrations may also facilitate the communication process.

Given the time constraints and the relatively challenging nature of oral presentations, even experienced researchers will conduct a series of practice presentations prior to delivery. This ensures that the presentation adheres to the time limit, and that any problems can be identified and eliminated.

10.16 Publishing in a Magazine

Unlike other academic disciplines, research in the aviation environment generally arises from problems within the operational environment. Consequently, there is an obligation on researchers to ensure that the outcomes of research are disseminated to those individuals who have the greatest stake in the research. One of the most effective means for disseminating this type of information is through industry-based magazine articles.

In some cases, researchers may elect to publish research outcomes in both a refereed journal and a magazine. This raises an important issue concerning the publication of the same work in more than one journal. From a legal perspective, any work that is submitted to a journal for publication typically becomes the property of the journal. Therefore, publishing the same article in a different journal amounts to a breach of copyright. To avoid the breach of copyright, the article must be completely rewritten and submitted to a journal that targets an audience distinct from the first publication. Consequently, the publication of research outcomes in both a refereed journal and a magazine article is usually acceptable.

There are a number of magazines available in which to publish research outcomes. Some of the more popular aviation magazines that are generally available include:

- Australian Aviation
- Pilot
- Flying
- Flight Training
- Australian Flying
- Aircraft and Aerospace
- Asian Aviation
- Business and Commercial Aviation
- International Society of Air Safety Investigators' Forum
- Flight Safety

Unlike refereed journals, magazine articles are written in a less formal style and do not include references. In addition, there is a significant reliance upon illustrations to accompany the material, and detailed statistical analyses should be avoided. Finally, magazine articles are relatively short (2,000 words) and some detail is normally discarded.

When writing magazine articles, references to previous work are normally embodied within the text of a magazine article. For example, 'Wickens (1992) asserts that...' might be replaced with 'Christopher Wickens from the University of Illinois suggests that...'. This reflects the more conversational style of writing that is employed in magazine articles, and that is designed to attract and hold attention for the duration of the article.

Consistent with refereed journals, magazine articles are generally unsolicited, and a prospective author is required to submit an article to an editor for consideration. When writing the article, it is extremely important to consider the characteristics of the readership, and whether or not there would be a level of interest in the article.

One of the main problems involved in magazine publications is that scholarly research is not necessarily timely. Therefore, an editor may accept an article, but reserve the article for a particular issue of the magazine. As a result, authors may wait some months to have an article published in an industry magazine.

From an academic perspective, it might be argued that magazine articles lack the rigour necessary for the publication of research outcomes. Clearly, there must be a place for the publication of research outcomes within the operational environment, using terminology that is appropriate for the particular context. Consequently, there is a need to strike a balance between the necessity for academic rigour in publications, and the requirement to publish outcomes in a format that is appropriate for the users of this information.

Publishing in a magazine generally amounts to a release of scientific information to media. As a result, it may be subjected to a level of misinterpretation that would not normally occur within the scientific community. Although this type of situation may be unavoidable, it highlights the principle that the outcomes of scientific research must be subjected to scientific peer review and comment prior to publication in an industry forum. This ensures that the information released to the public has, at least, a valid scientific basis.

10.17 Chapter Summary

This chapter was designed to facilitate the development of the skills necessary to publish the outcomes of research within a variety of outlets. These outlets ranged from refereed journals such as the *International Journal of Aviation Psychology* and *Aviation, Space and Environmental Medicine*, through to unrefereed magazine articles, such as *Flying*, and *Flight International*. Conference papers were also considered, and a number of practical techniques were provided to assist in the delivery of both presentations and posters.

10.18 Further Reading

American Psychological Association (1994). *The publication manual of the American Psychological Association* (4th ed.). Washington DC: Author.

Evans, D. (1996). *How to write a better thesis or report.* Melbourne, AUS: Melbourne University Press.

Locke, L.F., Spirduso, W. W., & Silverman, S.J. (1993). *Proposals that work: A guide for planning dissertations and grant proposals*. London, UK: Sage.

Sternberg, R.J. (1992). How to win acceptances by psychology journals: 21 tips for better writing. *APS Observer, 5,* 12-18.

11 Conclusion

Although aviation is a challenging environment, historically it represents one of the finest examples of a cooperative endeavour between humans and technology. From navigation to the structural components of aircraft, there have been consistent, significant improvements in the efficiency and accuracy of aircraft systems. However, there is one element of the aviation system, the components of which have remained relatively stable throughout this revolution.

Despite significant advances in aviation over recent years, the capabilities of the human designer and operator have remained stable. For example, the rate at which a human can process information, or the minimum distance at which a human can detect an oncoming aircraft will remain relatively consistent, irrespective of changes in technology. From a human factors perspective, the key is to ensure that there is an appropriate level of synergy between human capabilities and the functional characteristics of technology.

Even in the unlikely event of pilotless commercial airline transportation, the human can never be truly excluded from the aviation environment. The design and construction of systems will always be subject to some level of human intervention. Consequently, there remains an imperative to examine the relationship between humans and the operational environment in which they function.

Social science research comprises a series of strategies designed to facilitate an examination of the relationship between humans and the operational environment. It constitutes a series of principles and practises that are intended to ensure that research strategies are applied efficiently, ethically, and appropriately. In this book, we have sought to provide the foundation for an understanding of these principles as they apply within the aviation domain.

The book followed a relatively structured approach, consistent with the research process. It opened with a discussion concerning the nature of social science research and closed with the principles associated with the publication of research outcomes. The aim of this approach was to demonstrate that effective social science research is a structured, methodical process involving a relatively consistent sequence of procedures. However, at various junctures throughout the research process, the researcher is faced with a number of decisions, each of which involves a balance between a series of competing objectives. The role of the researcher is to consider the options and select a strategy that is likely to lead to the most appropriate outcome.

Making decisions in the face of uncertainty is a difficulty that faces both operational personnel and social science researchers within the aviation environment. In particular, the outcomes of research are far from clear, and errors can occur despite extensive preparation and planning. However, it is important to note that social science research, like any other research endeavour, does not always yield the desired results. The failure to obtain these results often requires a re-examination of the theoretical perspective from which the hypothesis or research question was derived, and/or the identification of any methodological limitations that may have occurred.

Throughout the book, an effort has been made to present the research process from a practical perspective. Examples were described to illustrate various issues, and decision trees were provided, where possible, to facilitate the decision-making process. In addition, a number of guidelines have been outlined to maximise the successful application of social science research techniques to the operational environment.

However, this practical approach to the research process should not be interpreted as tacit support for a phenomenon-driven approach that is devoid of a theoretical basis. Indeed, there will always be a temptation in applied research to conduct investigations in the absence of any detailed theoretical basis. Although this type of approach has some advantages from the perspective of descriptive research, it generally represents an inefficient approach to the development of solutions to applied problems. A much more effective strategy involves the development of appropriate theory that can subsequently be tested within the operational environment.

Having acquired additional information through experimentation, a theoretical perspective can be developed and modified as appropriate. The advantage of this type of approach is that, by understanding the fundamental processes through which humans function, solutions to other applied problems can also be developed without the additional costs associated with further experimental research.

Clearly, the development of universal knowledge is a distant goal for much of social science research. Nevertheless, it is a process that is consistent with the central theme of the scientific method. Debate and discussion of philosophical issues with respect to 'doing science' has provided a research strategy in which the ultimate reward is the acquisition of knowledge. However, it is also a cooperative endeavour in which different researchers contribute knowledge towards a common goal. Consequently, we have emphasised the publication of research results as an important responsibility for researchers.

Consistent with the theme of 'theory' and 'application' that occurs throughout, there is a focus on both the academic and industry-based publication of research outcomes. From the academic perspective, the publication is refereed and discussed by peers, and recommendations may be made prior to publication. From the industry-based perspective, a publication should be written in a form that meets the needs of readers. It should emphasise the applied outcomes of the research and the extent to which these outcomes will lead to improvements within the operational environment. The aim of this bipartite approach to publication is to ensure that important research findings are communicated as widely as possible to effect the maximum opportunity for change.

The opportunity for change within the aviation system has been an important motivator for the development of this book. It has been designed not only to provide guidance to researchers within the aviation industry, but also to encourage those practitioners who may have been toying with the idea of research to become a part of the initiative for improvement within the aviation environment. It is hoped that the book will also function as a catalyst for the development of appropriate research methodologies, and the publication of this information for the benefit of other researchers and practitioners. More specifically, our aim has been to generate a disciplined, cooperative approach to the analysis and explanation of human performance, in which researchers and practitioners function as a team to effect positive change within the complex, changing, and challenging aviation environment.

Glossary of Terms

After-Only Design An experimental design in which the comparisons are made between treatment groups.

Analysis of Variance (ANOVA) A commonly-used parametric statistical method for making simultaneous comparisons between two or more means (see also inferential statistics).

Applied Research Research in which the outcomes are specifically oriented towards solving problems within the operational environment.

Artefact, Experimental Errors arising from the process of experimentation (see Halo Effect, Audience Effect, Hawthorne Effect, and Serial-Order Effect).

Audience Effect An experimental bias caused by the presence of an observer.

Basic Research 'Pure' research in which the outcomes are specifically oriented towards understanding the nature of relationships between variables, irrespective of the application.

195

Before-After Design

An experimental design in which the comparisons are normally made between a group, prior to and post treatment or intervention (also referred to as a within-subjects design).

Categorical Data

Data that refer to categories or classes of information such as biological taxonomy, gender, language background of experimental participants (also referred to as nominal data).

Ceiling Effect

An experimental bias in which there is a tendency for responses to cluster at the higher end of a scale.

Central Tendency

The typical value of any distribution of scores. The mean, median and mode are all measures of central tendency.

Chi-Square

A non-parametric statistic that compares the observed frequency of the occurrence of some response or characteristic with the expected frequency. Chi-square provides a measure of association between categorical variables.

Conceptual Graph Analysis

A qualitative technique for data analysis in which nodes and actions are used to represent the cognitive and behavioural features of human performance in diagrammatic form.

Concept Map

A diagrammatic representation of the relationship between task-related components.

Construct

An underlying dimension or characteristic of a phenomenon (such as personality). A construct is often invoked to explain some relationship between two variables. For example, the capillary was a hypothetical construct until it was confirmed empirically by new medical technology.

Control (Experimental)

Refers to experimental designs and can relate to a control group that receives zero or 'normal' treatment. Extraneous factors that may influence the observed behaviour can also be subject to control by being held constant.

Correlation

A statistical measure that determines the strength of the relationship between two or more continuous variables. A perfect correlation is said to exist when systematic increases in the magnitude of one variable are accompanied by systematic increases (positive) or decreases (negative) in the magnitude of the other.

Counterbalancing

An experimental strategy to control for the influence of irrelevant factors. Counterbalancing the order of tasks in a two-task study involves exposing half the participants to Task 1 and then Task 2, and the other half of the sample to Task 2 and then Task 1.

Cross-Sectional Research

A research strategy in which data are acquired at a single point in time from a large sample that is expected to represent the breadth and diversity of a particular population.

Data

The plural form of datum. Datum is a fact assumed to be a matter of direct observation. Data then refers to the body of evidence or facts gathered in experiments or studies.

Data Types or Scales

Different measures of human performance yield different kinds of data, from scores on intelligence scales or attitude scales, to measures of accuracy or reaction time. The nature of the data or scale dictates the appropriate kind of statistical analysis that can be conducted. The four types of scales are nominal, ordinal, interval and ratio.

Degrees of Freedom

A statistical term that denotes that there are limits to the values that a researcher is free to choose given specific constraints.

Dependent Variable

A variable whose values are the result of changes in one or more independent variables. Often refers to participant's response or performance measured by the experimenter.

Double-Blind Strategy   An experimental technique where neither the data collector nor the participant are informed of the hypothesis or the experimental group to which the participant belongs.

Empirical Research   An approach to research that may be based on theory, but is verified by data, experiment and observation.

Factorial Design   An experimental design that is designed to determine the effect of all levels of one or more 'factors' (or independent variables) on one or more dependent variables.

Falsifiability   The philosophical notion that posits that scientific theories cannot be proven to be true, but only subject to attempts at refutation. In hypothesis testing, we attempt to reject the null hypothesis (that often specifies no relationship between variables) and, thereby, provide support for the alternative or experimental hypothesis.

Floor Effect   An experimental bias wherein there is a tendency for responses to cluster at the lower end of a scale.

Frequency Distribution

Any distribution based on a listing of the frequency of occurrences of the scores according to classes or categories. Each set of classes is marked with a number that represents its observed frequency. Any such display, whether in the form of a bar graph, frequency polygon or frequency curve, is referred to as a frequency distribution. The sum of the frequencies in a frequency distribution must equal N (the total number of scores).

Grounded Theory

A qualitative research technique that involves the description and subsequent analysis of phenomena as seen by those within the milieu.

Halo Effect

A research bias that occurs when observers attribute an overall impression of a person's performance to ratings of more specific attributes.

Hawthorne Effect

A research bias in which the observation process, rather than the experimental intervention, impacts upon the dependent variable (similar to the placebo effect).

Hypothesis

A statement of expectation pertaining to the nature of, or relationships between, variables.

Hypothetico-Deductive Method

See Scientific Method.

Independent Variable

An aspect of the environment that is manipulated systematically by the experimenter to determine whether it has an impact upon the dependent variable.

Inferential Statistics

The use of statistics to draw inferences: Probability theory is used to infer information about specific populations from sample data.

Interval Data

A measure in which the distance (or interval) between each unit is presumed to be equidistant (such as age). The distance between 30 and 40 years is the same as that between 50 and 60 years.

Longitudinal Research

Research in which observations of the same individuals are made over an extended period of time.

Mean (Arithmetic)

A measure of central tendency. A statistical term also referred to as the 'average'. The mean is calculated by summing the values in a data set and dividing by the number of values.

Median

A measure of central tendency. A statistical term referring to the middle number in a series of ranked or ordered values.

Mode

A measure of central tendency. A statistical term referring to the most frequently occurring number in a data set.

Nominal Data

See Categorical Data.

Non-Parametric Statistics A set of statistical methods that may be employed if the data do not meet the requirements for the application of parametric statistics. Non-parametric statistics are useful if the sample is small, or if the values are not normally distributed. They are also referred to as distribution-free statistical tests as they can be used without making assumptions about particular parameters of distributions.

Normal Distribution A symmetrical and unimodal distribution of values in which the mean, the median, and the mode coincide (also referred to as Gaussian Distribution).

Normative Data Pertains to norms or standards. A set of normative data is collected for the purpose of establishing norms and getting a sense of the underlying distribution.

Null Hypothesis A hypothesis set in opposition to the experimental hypothesis usually specifiying no difference or no relationship.

Ordinal Data Data that embody mutually exclusive categories within a ranked structure (such as preferences) or along some dimension.

Parametric Statistics   A class of statistical tests that are dependent upon the satisfaction of a series of assumptions including that the scores are normally-distributed.

Placebo Effect   Improved performance that results from participation in the study, expectation, or motivation, rather than being the result of the manipulation of the independent variable (see Hawthorne effect).

Population   All the cases of the phenomenon under investigation.

Probability   The likelihood of an event.

Probability Distribution   A distribution based on a listing of classes or categories paired with its probability of occurrence. The sum of the probabilities in a probability distribution must total 1.0.

Process Tracing   A qualitative research technique in which cognitive functions are inferred by 'tracing' the behaviour of participants.

Projection   A research bias in which a researcher ascribes attributes, perceptions or behaviours to participants in the absence of direct evidence of their relevance.

Protocol Analysis   A qualitative research technique that involves the verbalisation of human thought processes during or after the performance of a task.

Quasi-Experimental Research — A class of research strategies that includes aspects of both non-experimental and experimental research techniques.

Randomisation — A sample that is selected from a population in such a way that all the individuals have equal probability of being selected.

Range — The distance between the highest point and the lowest point in a distribution. The range is a measure of scores of variability.

Ratio Data — Data that embody mutually exclusive categories within a ranked structure, have equal spacing between the categories, and have an absolute zero point. Weight is an example of a ratio scale.

Reliability — The capability of an instrument to yield consistent results each time it is applied.

Repeated-Measures Design — An experimental design wherein participants receive two or more values of the independent variable.

Sample — An observed sub-set of a population.

A systematic and serial process of inquiry involving the acquisition and analysis of information, and the deduction and testing of hypotheses related to a particular phenomenon.

Serial-Order Effect

A research bias in which trials or responses early in the experimental sequence influence later trials and responses.

Skewness

The degree to which a curve of a frequency distribution departs from perfect symmetry. Skewness is either positive (to the right) or negative (to the left), depending on whether the tail of the distribution extends towards those values, relative to the mode.

Social Desirability

A research bias in which there is a tendency for a participant to give socially acceptable or expected responses.

Standard Deviation

A measure of the variability of scores around the mean of the sample. It is calculated as the average deviation of the scores from the mean value of the data set.

Statistic

A value computed from observations of a sample taken from a population. A sample mean, for example, is denoted $\overline{X}$.

Statistical Significance

The probability that a particular value is obtained, given the value as specified in the null hypothesis.

Thematic Approach

A qualitative research technique that involves the development of factors or themes that underlie the information obtained from participants.

t-test

A parametric statistical test designed to determine the difference between two independent or matched experimental groups.

Type I Error

A statistical error in which the null hypothesis is rejected in favour of the experimental hypothesis when, in fact, the null hypothesis is true.

Type II Error

A statistical error in which the null hypothesis is accepted in favour of the experimental hypothesis when, in fact, it is false.

Validity

The extent to which an instrument measures the construct that it is designed to measure.

Variable

Any value that has the capability to vary (such as age or height).

Variance

The standard deviation squared. It is a measure of dispersion or the variability of a set of scores (see also Analysis of Variance).

World-Wide Web

The communications system created by interconnecting networks of computers around the world.

References

Adelman, L., Cohen, M.S., Bresnick, T.A., Chinnis, J.O., & Laskey, K.B. (1993). Real-time expert systems interfaces, cognitive processes and task performance: An empirical assessment. *Human Factors, 35,* 243-261.

Aiken, L.R. (1979). *Psychological testing and assessment* (3rd ed.). Boston, MA: Allyn & Bacon.

American Psychological Association. (1994). *Publication manual* (4th ed.). Washington, DC: Author.

American Psychological Association. (1992). Ethical principles of psychologists and code of conduct. *American Psychologist, 47,* 1597-1611.

Anderson, P.M. (1993). *Problem-based learning and the development of team skills in aviation studies.* Unpublished honours thesis, University of Newcastle, Newcastle, Australia.

Ball, L.J., Evans, J.St.B.T., & Dennis, I. (1994). Cognitive processes in engineering design: A longitudinal study. *Ergonomics, 37,* 1753-1786.

Banaji, M.R., & Crowder, R.G. (1989). The bankruptcy of everyday memory. *American Psychologist, 44,* 1185-1193.

Barratt, P.E.H. (1971). *Bases of psychological methods.* Brisbane, AUS: Wiley.

Baumrind, D. (1964). Some thoughts on ethics of research: After reading Milgram's "Behavioural study of obedience". *American Psychologist, 19,* 421-423.

Becker, A.S., Warm, J.S., Dember, W.N., & Hancock, P.A. (1995). Effects of jet engine noise and performance feedback on perceived workload in a monitoring task. *The International Journal of Aviation Psychology, 5,* 49-62.

Beringer, D.B., & Harris, H.C. (1997). *Automation in general aviation: Two studies of pilot responses to autopilot malfunctions.* Washington, D.C.: Federal Aviation Administration (NTIS DOT/FAA/AM-97/24).

Billings, C.E., & Reynard, W.D. (1984). Human factors in aircraft incidents: Results of a 7-year study. *Aviation, Space, and Environmental Medicine, 55,* 960-965.

Bordens, K.S., & Abbott, B.B. (1991). *Research design and methods: A process approach* (2nd ed.). Mountain View, CA: Mayfield Publishing.

Bowers, C., Deaton, J., Oser, R., Prince, C., & Kolb, M. (1995). Impact of automation on aircrew performance and decision-making performance. *The International Journal of Aviation Psychology, 5,* 145-168.

Brannen, J. (1992). Combining qualitative and quantitative approaches: An overview. In J. Brannen (Ed.), *Mixing methods: Qualitative and quantitative research.* Aldershot, UK: Avebury.

Braune, R., Stokes, A., & Wickens, C.D. (1985). An exploratory study of computer-based aviation testing. In R.S. Jensen & J. Adrion (Eds.), *Proceedings of the Third International Symposium on Aviation Psychology* (pp. 521-528). Columbus, OH: Ohio State University Press.

Bruggink, G.M. (1998, October/December). A changing accident pattern. *ISASI Forum, 25*-27.

Bryan, S.J. (1997). Cognitive and motivational factors influencing time prediction. *Journal of Experimental Psychology: Applied, 3,* 216-239.

Bryman, A. (1988). *Quantity and quality in social research.* London, UK: Unwin Hyman.

Bryman, A. (1992). Quantitative and qualitative research: Further reflections on integration. In J. Brannen (Ed.), *Mixing methods: Qualitative and quantitative research* (pp. 57-78). Aldershot, UK: Avebury.

Bryman, A., & Cramer, C. (1994). *Quantitative data analysis for social scientists.* London, UK: Routledge.

Bulmer, M. (1979). Concepts in the analysis of qualitative data. *Sociological Review, 27,* 651-677.

Bureau of Air Safety Investigation. (1991). *Accident Investigation Report: Gulfstream Aerospace AC 681 VH-NYG, Tamworth, NSW, 14 February, 1991* (B/911/1012). Canberra, AUS: Department of Transport & Communications.

Burke, E., Hobson, C., & Linsky, C. (1997). Large sample validations of three general predictors of pilot training success. *The International Journal of Aviation Psychology, 7,* 225-234.

Butcher, J.N., & Hatcher, C. (1988). The neglected entity in air disaster planning. *American Psychologist, 43,* 724-729.

Carmigniani, V., & Palayret, B. (1989). Exploratory experience in mental process in some airplane accidents due to human factors. In R.S. Jensen (Ed.), *Proceedings of the Fifth International Symposium on Aviation Psychology* (pp. 860-865). Columbus, OH: Ohio State University Press.

Carroll, J.S., & Johnson, E.J. (1990). *Decision research: A field guide.* Newbury Park, CA: Sage Publications.

Chalmers, A.F. (1988). *What is this thing called science?* (2nd ed.). St. Lucia, AUS: University of Queensland Press.

Christensen, L.B. (1991). *Experimental methodology* (5th ed.). Boston, MA: Allyn & Bacon.

Civil Aviation Safety Authority. (1995). *Aviation regulatory proposal* (ARP 1/95). Canberra, AUS: Author.

Coffey, A., & Atkinson, P. (1996). *Making sense of qualitative data.* Thousand Oaks, CA: Sage.

Cohen, L., & Manion, L. (1986). *Research methods in education.* London, UK: Croom Helm.

Cooke, N. (1994). Varieties of knowledge elicitation techniques. *The International Journal of Human-Computer Studies, 41,* 801-849.

Cooper, W.H. (1981). Ubiquitous halo. *Psychological Bulletin, 90,* 218-244.

Crowne, D.P., & Marlowe, D. (1964). *The approval motive.* New York, NY: Wiley.

Diamond, M.R., & Reidpath, D.D. (1992). Psychology ethics down under: A survey of student subject pools in Australia. *Ethics and Behaviour, 2,* 101-108.

Dingus, T.A., McGehee, D.V., Manakkal, N., Jahns, S.K., Carney, C., & Hankey, J.M. (1997). Human factors field evaluation of automotive headway maintenance/collision warning devices. *Human Factors, 39,* 216-229.

Drake, S. (Ed.). (1957). *Discoveries and opinions of Galileo.* Garden City, NY: Anchor.

Dreyfus, H.L. & Dreyfus, S.E. (1986). Why skills cannot be represented by rules. In N.E. Sharley (Ed.), *Advances in cognitive science 1* (pp. 315-335). Chichester: Ellis Harwood.

Dutke, S. (1994). Error handling: Visualisations in the human-computer interface and exploratory learning. *Applied Psychology: An International Review, 43,* 521-541.

Dyer, C. (1995). *Beginning research in psychology.* Oxford, UK: Blackwell.

Eckstrand, G.A. (1964). *Current status of the technology of training.* Report AMRL-TDR-64-86. Aerospace Medical Laboratories, Wright-Patterson Air Force Base.

Ericsson, K.A., & Simon, H.A. (1996). *Protocol analysis: verbal reports as data.* Cambridge, MA: MIT Press.

Esser, J.K., & Lindoerfer, J.S. (1989). Groupthink and the space Challenger accident: Toward a quantitative case analysis. *Journal of Behavioural Decision-Making, 2,* 167-177.

Fairbank, J.A., Jordan, B.K., & Schlenger, W.E. (1996). Designing and implementing epidemiologic studies. In E.B. Carlson (Ed.), *Trauma research methodology* (pp. 105-125). Lutherville, MD: Sidron.

Feldman, J.M. (1986). A note on the statistical correlation of halo error. *Journal of Applied Psychology, 71,* 173-176.

Feyerabend, P.K. (1975). *Aganist method: Outline of an anarchistic theory of knowledge.* London, UK: New Left Books.

Fisk, A.D., & Gallini, J.K. (1989). Training consistent components of tasks: Developing an instructional system based on automatic/controlled processing principles. *Human Factors, 31,* 453-463.

Flanagan, J.C. (1954). The critical incident technique. *Psychological Bulletin, 51,* 327-358.

Garriba, S.F. (1986). The use of weak information structures in risky decisions. In E. Hollnagel, G. Mancini, & D.D. Woods, (Eds.), *Intelligent decision support in process environments* (pp. 39-44). Berlin, WG: Springer-Verlag.

Giffen, W.C., & Rockwell, T.H. (1984). Computer-aided testing of pilot response to critical in-flight events. *Human Factors, 26,* 573-581.

Glendinning, A., Shucksmith, J., & Hendry, L. (1994). Social class and adolescent smoking behaviour. *Social Science & Medicine, 38,* 1449-1460.

Godwin, J.L., & Neck, C.P. (1996). Researcher 'projection' revisited: A response to Kahn. *Journal of Applied Behavioral Science, 32,* 323-331.

Goldstein, I.L. (1978). The pursuit of validity in the evaluation of training programs. *Human Factors, 20,* 131-144.

Gordon, S.E., Schmierer, K.A., Gill, R.T. (1993). Conceptual graph analysis: Knowledge acquisition for instructional system design. *Human Factors, 35,* 459-481.

Gottfredson, G.D. (1996). The Hawthorne misunderstanding (and how to get the Hawthorne effect in action research). *Journal of Research in Crime and Delinquency, 33,* 28-48.

Gregorich, S.E., Helmreich, R.L., & Wilhelm, J.A. (1990). The structure of cockpit managment attitudes. *Journal of Applied Psychology, 75,* 682-690.

Haber, R.N. (1987). Why low-flying fighter planes crash: Perceptual and attentional factors in collisions with the ground. *Human Factors, 29,* 519-532.

Haney, C., Banks, W.C., & Zimbardo, P.G. (1973). A study of prisoners and guards in a simulated prison. *Naval Research Review, 30,* 4-17.

Harré, R., Gundlach, H.U.K., Métraux, A., Ockwell, A., & Wilkes, K.V. (1985). Antagonism and interaction: The relations of philosophy to psychology. In C.E. Buxton (Ed.), *Points of view in the modern history of psychology* (pp. 383-415). Orlando, FL: Academic Press.

Harris, D. (1991). The importance of the Type II error in aviation safety research. In E.Farmer (Ed.), *Stress and error in aviation.* Aldershot, UK: Avebury.

Harwood, K., Murphy, E., & Roske-Hofstrand, R. (1991). Exploring conceptual structures in air traffic control. In R.S. Jensen (Ed.), *Proceedings of the Sixth International Symposium of Aviation Psychology* (pp. 466-473). Columbus, OH: Ohio State University Press.

Hedrick, T.E., Bickman, L., & Rog, D.J. (1993). *Applied research design: A practical guide.* Newbury Park, CA: Sage.

Helmreich, R.L. (1984). Cockpit management attitudes. *Human Factors, 26,* 583-589.

Helmreich, R.L. (1987). Exploring flight crew behaviour. *Social Behaviour, 2,* 63-72.

Helmreich, R.L. (1994). Anatomy of a system accident: The crash of Avianca Flight 052. *The International Journal of Aviation Psychology, 4,* 265-284.

Helmreich, R.L., & Davies, J.M. (1997). Anaesthetic simulation and lessons to be learned from aviation. *Canadian Journal of Anaesthesiology, 44,* 907-912.

Helmreich, R.L., & Wilhelm, J.A. (1991). Outcomes of crew resource training. *The International Journal of Aviation Psychology, 1,* 287-300.

Henley, I. (1991). The development and evaluation of flight instructors: A descriptive survey. *The International Journal of Aviation Psychology, 1,* 319-333.

Henley, I. (1995). *The quality of the development and evaluation of flight instructors in Canada and Australia.* Unpublished doctoral dissertation, University of Newcastle, Newcastle, Australia.

Hess, R.A. (1987). A qualitative model of human interaction with complex dynamic systems. *IEEE Transactions on Systems, Man, and Cybernetics, SMC-17,* 33-51.

Hoffman, R.R. (1987). The problem of extracting the knowledge of experts from the perspective of experimental psychology. *AI Magazine, 8,* 53-67.

Hogarth, R.M., Gibbs, B.J., McKenzie, C.R.M., & Marquis, M.A. (1991). Learning from feedback: Exactingness and incentives. *Journal of Experimental Psychology: Learning, Memory, and Cognition, 17,* 734-752.

Howell, D.C. (1989). *Fundamental statistics for the behavioural sciences.* Boston, MA: PWS-Kent.

Howell, D.C. (1997). *Statistical methods for psychology* (4th ed.). Belmont, CA: Duxbury Press.

Hull, C.L. (1943). *Principles of behaviour.* New York, NY: Appleton-Century-Crofts.

Hull, J.C., Gill, R.T., & Roscoe, S.N. (1982). Locus of the stimulus to visual accommodation: Where in the world, or where is the eye? *Human Factors, 24,* 311-319.

Hunter, D.R. (1995). *Airman Research Questionnaire: Methodology and Overall Results.* Washington, DC: Federal Aviation Administration (NTIS DOT/FAA/AM-95/27).

Hunter, D.R., & Burke, E.F. (1994). Predicting aircraft pilot-training success: A meta-analysis of published research. *The International Journal of Aviation Psychology, 4,* 297-314.

Hunter, J.E., & Schmidt, F.L. (1990). *Methods of meta-analysis: Correcting error and bias in research findings.* Newbury Park, CA: Sage.

Iavecchia, J.H., Iavecchia, H.P., & Roscoe, S.N. (1988). Eye accommodation to head-up virtual images. *Human Factors 30,* 689-702.

Isaac, A.R. (1994). Imagery ability and air traffic personnel. *Aviation, Space, and Environmental Medicine, 65,* 95-99.

Janis, I.L. (1983). *Groupthink.* Boston, MA: Houghton Mifflin.

Jung, J. (1971). *The experimenter's dilemma.* New York, NY: Harper & Row.

Kachigan, S.K. (1991). *Multivariate statistical analysis: A conceptual introduction.* New York, NY: Radius Press.

Kaempf, G.L., Wolf, S.P., Thordsen, M.L., & Klein, G. (1992). *Decision-making in the Aegis combat information centre* (Naval Command, Control and Ocean Surveillance Centre Report N66001-90-C-6023). San Diego, CA: Klein Associates.

Kahn, W.A. (1996). Comment on "Understanding researcher 'projection' in interpreting case study data: The South Canyon Fire Tragedy". *Journal of Applied Behavioral Science, 32,* 62-69.

Kanki, B.G., & Foushee, H.C. (1989). Communication as group mediator of aircrew performance. *Aviation, Space and Environmental Medicine, 60,* 402-410.

Kerlinger, F.N. (1979). *Behavioural research: A conceptual approach.* New York, NY: Holt, Rinehart & Wilson.

Kerlinger, F.N. (1992). *Foundations of behavioural research* (3rd ed.). Fort Worth, TX: Harcourt Brace College.

Kimmel, A.J. (1996). *Ethical issues in behavioural research.* Cambridge, MA: Blackwell.

Kirk, R.E. (1968). *Experimental design: Procedures for the behavioural sciences.* Belmont, CA: Brooks/Cole.

Kirschenbaum, S.S. (1992). Influence of experience on information-search strategies. *Journal of Applied Psychology, 77,* 343-352.

Klein, G.A. (1989). Recognition-primed decisions (RPD*). Advances in Man-Machine Systems, 5,* 47-92.

Klein, G., & Klinger, D. (1991). Naturalistic decision making. *Crew System Ergonomics Information Analysis Centre Newsletter, 2,* 1-4.

Klein, G.A. (1990). Using knowledge engineering to preserve corporate memory. In R.R. Hoffman (Ed.), *The psychology of expertise* (pp.170-187). New York, NY: Springer-Verlag.

Klein, G.A., Calderwood, R., & MacGregor, D. (1989). Critical decision method for eliciting knowledge. *IEEE Transactions on Systems, Man, and Cybernetics, 19,* 462-472.

Koelega, H.S., & Brinkman, J.A. (1986). Noise and vigilance: An evaluative review. *Human Factors, 28,* 465-481.

Koonce, J.M. (1984). A brief history of aviation psychology. *Human Factors, 26,* 499-508.

Koubek, R.J., Salvendy, G., & Noland, S. (1994). The use of protocol analysis for determining ability requirements for personnel selection on a computer-based task. *Ergonomics, 37,* 1787-1800.

Kraft, C.L. (1978). A psychophysiological contribution to air safety: Simulator studies of visual illusions in night visual approaches. In H. Pick, H.W. Leibowitz, J.R. Singer, A. Steinschneider, & H.W. Stevenson (Eds.), *Psychology from research to practice* (pp. 363-385). New York, NY: Plenum.

Kruithof, J., & Ryall, J. (1994). *The quality standards handbook.* Melbourne, AUS: The Business Library.

Kuhn, T.S. (1970). *The structure of scientific revolutions.* Chicago, IL: Chicago University Press.

Lance, C.E., Lapointe, J.A., & Stewart, A.M. (1994). A test of the context dependency of three causal models of halo rater error. *Journal of Applied Psychology, 79,* 332-340.

Laudan, L. (1994). *The book of risks.* New York, NY: John Wiley & Sons.

Leach, J. (1991). *Running applied psychology experiments.* Bristol, PA: Open University Press.

Lee, A.T. (1991). Aircrew decision-making behaviour in hazardous weather avoidance. *Aviation, Space, and Environmental Medicine, 62,* 158-161.

Li, G., & Baker, S.P. (1997). Injury patterns in aviation-related fatalities: Implications for preventative strategies. *The American Journal of Forensic Medicine and Pathology, 18,* 265-270.

Lintern, G., & Garrison, W.V. (1992). Transfer effects of scene content and crosswind in landing instruction. *The International Journal of Aviation Psychology, 2,* 225-244.

Lloyd, P., Mayes, A., Manstead, A.S.R., Meudell, P.R., & Wagner, H.L. (1990). *Introduction to psychology: An integrated approach.* London, UK: Fontana Press.

Loftus, E.F., & Palmer, J.C. (1974). Reconstruction of auto-mobile destruction: An example of the interaction between language and memory. *Journal of Verbal Learning and Verbal Behaviour, 13,* 585-589.

Macarthur, R.D., & Sekuler, R. (1982). Alcohol and motion perception. *Perception & Psychophysics, 31,* 502-505.

McFarland, M.W. (1953). *The papers of Wilbur and Orville Wright, including the Chanute-Wright letters and other papers of Octave Chanute.* New York, NY: McGraw-Hill.

McGuigan, F.J. (1997). *Experimental psychology: Methods of research* (7th ed.). New Jersey, NJ: Prentice Hall.

McLean, G.A., Palmerton, D.A., Chittum, C.B., George, M.H., & Funkhouser, G.H. (1998). *Inflatable escape slide beam and girt strength tests: Support for revision of TSO C-69b.* Washington, DC: Federal Aviation Administration. (NTIS DOT/FAA/AM-98/3).

Martinussen, M. (1996). Psychological measures as predictors of pilot performance: A meta-analysis. *The International Journal of Aviation Psychology, 6,* 1-20.

Mathison, S. (1988, March). Why triangulate? *Educational Researcher,* 13-17.

Maurino, D.F., Reason, J., Johnston, N., & Lee, R.B. (1995). *Beyond aviation human factors.* Aldershot, UK: Avebury Aviation.

Means, B. (1993). Cognitive task analysis as a basis for instructional design. In M. Rabinowitz (Ed.), *Cognitive science foundations of instruction* (pp. 97-118). Hillsdale, NJ: Lawrence Erlbaum.

Meehan, J.W., & Triggs, T.J. (1992). Apparent size and distance in an imaging display. *Human Factors, 34,* 303-311.

Merritt, A., & Helmreich, R.L. (1996). Human factors on the flight deck: The influence of national culture. *Journal of Cross-Cultural Psychology, 27,* 5-24.

Miles, M.B., & Huberman, A.M. (1994). *Qualitative data analysis* (2nd ed.). Thousand Oaks, CA: Sage.

Milgram, S. (1963). Behavioural study of obedience. *Journal of Abnormal and Social Psychology. 67,* 371-378.

Milgram, S. (1964a). Group pressure and action against a person. *Journal of Abnormal and Social Psychology, 69,* 137-143.

Milgram, S. (1964b). Issues in the study of obedience: A reply to Baumrind. *American Psychologist, 19,* 848-852.

Minium, E.W., King, B.M., & Bear, G. (1993). *Statistical reasoning in psychology and education* (3rd ed.). New York, NY: Wiley.

Mitchell, M., & Jolley, J. (1992). *Research design explained* (2nd ed.). Forth Worth, TX: Harcourt Brace Jovanovich.

Monette, D.R., Sullivan, T.J., & DeJong, C.R. (1986). *Applied social research.* Fort Worth, TX: Holt, Rinehart & Winston.

Mosier, K.L. (1991). Expert decision-making. In R.S. Jensen (Ed.), *Proceedings of the Sixth International Symposium on Aviation Psychology* (pp. 266-271). Columbus, OH: Ohio State University.

Muir, H.C. (1994). Passenger safety. In N. Johnston, N. McDonald, & R. Fuller (Eds.), *Aviation psychology in practice* (pp. 105-124). Aldershot, UK: Ashgate.

Muir, H.C., Bottomley, D.M., & Marrison, C. (1996). Effects of motivation and cabin configuration on emergency behaviour and rates of egress. *The International Journal of Aviation Psychology, 6,* 57-77.

Murphy, K.R., Jako, R.A., & Anhalt, R.L. (1993). Nature and consequences of halo error: A critical analysis. *Journal of Applied Psychology, 78,* 218-225.

Nakagawara, V.B., & Wood, K.J. (1996). *The use of task-specific lenses by presbyopic air traffic controllers at the en-route radar console.* Washington, DC: US Department of Transportation. (NTIS DOT/FAA/AM-96/27).

National Health & Medical Research Council. (1992). *Statement on human experimentation and supplementary notes.* Canberra, AUS: Australian Government Publishing Service.

National Transportation Safety Board. (1979). *Aircraft Accident Report - United Airlines, Inc., McDonnell Douglas DC-8-61, N8082U, Portland, Oregon, December 28, 1978.* Washington, DC: Author.

National Transportation Safety Board. (1990a). *Aircraft Accident Report - United Airlines Flight 811, Boeing 747-122, N4713U, Honolulu, Hawaii, February 24, 1989.* Washington, DC: Author.

National Transportation Safety Board. (1990b). *Aircraft Accident Report – United Airlines Flight 232, McDonnell Douglas DC-10-10, Sioux Gateway Airport, Sioux City, Iowa, July 19, 1989.* Washington, DC: Author.

Neck, C.P., Godwin, J.L., & Spencer, E.S. (1996). Understanding researcher 'projection' in interpreting case study data: The South Canyon Fire Tragedy. *Journal of Applied Behavioral Science, 32,* 48-61.

Nisbett, R.E., & Wilson, T.D. (1977). Telling more than we can know: Verbal reports on mental processes. *Psychological Review, 84,* 231-259.

O'Hare, D., Wiggins, M., Batt, R., & Morrison, D. (1994). Cognitive failure analysis for aircraft accident investigation. *Ergonomics, 37,* 1855-1869.

Ortiz, G.A. (1994). Effectiveness of PC-based flight simulation. *The International Journal of Aviation Psychology, 4,* 285-291.

Oster, C.V., Strong, J.S., & Zorn, C.K. (1992). *Why airplanes crash*. New York, NY: Oxford University Press.

Ostrom, T.M., Skowronski, J.J., & Nowak, A. (1994). The cognitive foundation of attitudes: It's a wonderful construct. In P.G. Devine, D.L. Hamilton, & T.M. Ostrom (Eds.), *Social cognition: Impact on social psychology* (pp. 195-258). San Diego, CA: Academic Press.

Patrick, J. (1991). Types of analysis for training. In J.E. Morrison (Ed.), *Training for Performance: Principles of Applied Human Learning* (pp.127-166). New York, NY: Wiley.

Pengilley, W., & McPhee, J. (1994). *Law for aviators*. Sydney, AUS: Legal Books.

Perrott, D.R., Cisneros, J., McKinley, R.L., & D'Angelo, W.R. (1996). Aurally aided visual search under virtual and free-field listening conditions. *Human Factors, 38*, 702-715.

Peshkin, A. (1993). The goodness of qualitative research. *Educational Researcher, 22*, 24-30.

Petrie, K.J., & Dawson, A.G. (1997). Symptoms of fatigue and coping strategies in international pilots. *The International Journal of Aviation Psychology, 7*, 251-258.

Phillips, E.D. (1996, November 4). Legal problems cloud airline safety programs. *Aviation Week and Space Technology*, 66-68.

Pitman, M.A., & Maxwell, J.A. (1992). Qualitative approaches to evaluation: Models and Methods. In M.D. LeCompte, W.L. Millroy, & J. Preissle (Eds.), *The handbook of qualitative research in education* (pp. 729-770). San Diego, CA: Academic Press.

Popper, K. (1969). *Conjectures and refutations*. London, UK: Routledge & Kegan Paul.

Rains, A.J.H. (1974). *Edward Jenner and vaccination*. London, UK: Priory Press.

Rasmussen, J. (1990). Mental models and the control of action in complex environments. In D. Ackerman & M.J. Tauber (Eds.), *Mental models and human-computer interaction* (pp. 41-69). North Holland, NL: Elsevier Sciences.

Ratner, R.S., & Guselli, J. (1995). Techniques for identifying indirect causal factors in aviation incidents and accidents. *ISASI Forum, 28*, 7-20.

Reason, J.T. (1990). *Human error*. Cambridge, UK: Cambridge University Press.

Redding, R.E., Ryder, J.M., Seamster, T.L., Purcell, J.A., and Cannon, J.R. (1991). *Cognitive task analysis of en-route air traffic control: Model extension and validation*, Report to the Federal Aviation Administration, McLean, VA, Human Technology Inc. (ERIC Document Reproduction Service. No. ED 340 848).

Redding, R.E., & Seamster, T.L. (1994). Cognitive task analysis in air traffic controller and aviation crew training. In N. Johnston, N. McDonald, & R. Fuller (Eds.), *Aviation psychology in practice* (pp. 190-222). Aldershot, UK: Avebury.

Robson, C. (1994). *Experiment, design and statistics in psychology* (4th ed.). Harmondsworth, UK: Penguin.

Roethlisberger, F.J., & Dickson, W.J. (1939). *Management and the worker.* Cambridge, MA: Harvard University Press.

Roscoe, S.N. (1979). When day is done and shadows fall, we miss the airport most of all. *Human Factors, 21,* 721-731.

Roscoe, S.N. (1982). Landing airplanes, detecting traffic, and the dark focus. *Aviation, Space, and Environmental Medicine, 53,* 970-976.

Rosnow, R.L., & Rosenthal, R. (1997). *People studying people: Artifacts and ethics in behavioural research.* New York, NY: W.H. Freeman.

Rouse, W.B., & Vasulek, J. (1993). Evolutionary design of systems to support decision-making. In G.A. Klein, J. Orasanu, R. Calderwood, & C.E. Zsambok (Eds.), *Decision making in action: models and methods* (p. 270-286). Norwood, NJ: Ablex.

Rowntree, D. (1991). *Statistics without tears: A primer for non-mathematicians.* London, UK: Penguin.

Ryder, J.M., & Redding, R.E. (1993). Integrating cognitive task analysis into instructional systems development. *Educational Technology Research and Development, 41,* 75-96.

Salvatore, S., Stearns, M.D., Huntley, M.S., & Mengert, P. (1986). Air transport pilot involvement in general aviation accidents. *Ergonomics, 29,* 1455-1467.

Sanderson, P.M., James, J.M., & Seidler, K.S. (1989). SHAPA: an interactive software environment for protocol analysis. *Ergonomics, 32,* 1271-1302.

Sanderson, P., Scott, J., Johnston, T., Mainzer, J., Watanabe, L., & James, J. (1994). MacSHAPA and the enterprise of exploratory sequential data analysis. *The International Journal of Human-Computer Studies, 41,* 633-681.

Schlager, M.S., Means, B., & Roth, C. (1990). Cognitive task analysis for the real - time world. *Proceedings of the Human Factors Society, 34th Annual Meeting* (pp. 1309-1313). Santa Monica, CA, Human Factors Society.

Seamster, T.L., Redding, R.E., & Kaempf, G.L. (1997). *Applied cognitive task analysis in aviation.* Aldershot, UK: Avebury Technical.

Shappell, S.A., & Wiegmann, D.A. (1997). A human error approach to accident investigation: The taxonomy of unsafe operations. *The International Journal of Aviation Psychology, 7,* 269-292.

Sherman, P.J., & Helmreich, R.L. (1993). *The controller resource management attitudes questionnaire (CRMAQ): Review methodology, results* (NASA/UT/FAA Technical Report 93-1). Austin, TX: University of Texas.

Siegel, S., & Castellan, N.J. (1988). *Non-parametric statistics for the behavioural sciences* (2nd ed.). New York, NY: McGraw-Hill.

Simpson, P., & Wiggins, M. (1996). Human factors attitudes. In B.J. Hayward & A.R. Lowe (Eds.), *Applied aviation psychology: Achievement, change and challenge* (pp. 185-192). Aldershot, UK: Ashgate.

Smith, G., Meehan, J.W., & Day, R.H. (1992). The effect of accommodation on retinal image size. *Human Factors, 34,* 289-301.

Smith, G.M. (1995). Active-learning strategies in undergraduate CRM flight training. In N. Johnston, R. Fuller, & N. McDonald (Eds.), *Aviation psychology: Training and selection* (pp. 17-22). Aldershot, UK: Avebury Aviation.

Solso, R.L., & Johnson, H.H. (1984). *An introduction to experimental design in psychology: A case approach* (3rd ed.). New York, NY: Harper & Row.

Sommer, R., & Sommer, B.B. (1980). *A practical guide to behavioural research.* New York, NY: Oxford University Press.

Sowa, J.F. (1990). Conceptual analysis as a basis for knowledge acquisition. In R.R. Hoffman (Ed.), *The psychology of expertise* (pp 80-96). New York, NY: Springer-Verlag.

Spatz, C., & Johnston, J.O. (1989). *Basic statistics: Tales of distributions.* Pacific Grove, CA: Brooks/Cole.

Steinberg, L. (1994). Context and serial-order effects in personality measurement: Limits on the generality of measuring changes in measures. *Journal of Personality and Social Psychology, 66,* 341-349.

Stone, R.B., & Young, S.T. (1997, April/June). How active is the Board Room in preventing accidents? *ISASI Forum,* 5-9.

Strauss, A. (1987). *Qualitative analysis for social scientists.* Cambridge, UK: Cambridge University Press.

Strauss, A., & Corbin, J. (1990). *Basics of qualitative research.* Newbury Park, CA: Sage.

Svenson, O. (1989). Eliciting and analysing verbal protocols in process studies of judgement and decision making. In H. Montgomery & O. Svenson (Eds.), *Process and structure in human decision-making* (pp. 65-81). Chichester, UK: John Wiley & Sons.

Tabachnick, B.G., & Fidell, L.S. (1996). *Using multivariate statistics* (3rd ed.). New York, NY: Harper Collins.

Thordsen, M.L. (1991). A comparison of two tools for cognitive task analysis: Concept mapping and the critical decision method. *Proceedings of the Human Factors Society 35th Annual Meeting* (pp. 283-285). Santa Monica, CA: Human Factors and Ergonomics Society.

Tirre, W.C., & Raouf, K.K. (1994). Gender differences in perceptual-motor performance. *Aviation, Space and Environmental Medicine, 65,* A49-A53.

Ungs, T.J. (1994). Civil aviation mortality, state differences, and the role of multi-fatality aircraft accidents. *Aviation, Space and Environmental Medicine, 65,* 546-550.

University of Chicago. (1993). *Chicago Manual of Style.* Chicago, IL: University of Chicago Press.

218   *Aviation Social Science: Research Methods in Practice*

Urban, J.M., Weaver, J.L., Bowers, C.A., & Rhodenizer, L. (1996). Effects of workload and structure on team processes and performance: Implications for complex team decision-making. *Human Factors, 38,* 300-312.

Wiener, E.L. (1993). *Intervention strategies for the management of human error.* (Report No. 4547). Moffett Field, CA: National Aeronautics & Space Administration.

Wiggins, M.W., & Henley, I. (1997). A computer-cased analysis of expert and novice flight instructor pre-flight decision-making. *The International Journal of Aviation Psychology, 7,* 365-379.

Wiggins, M., Henley, I., Foley, S., & Moore, P. (1996). Expert versus novice flight instruction. In B.J. Hayward, & A.R. Lowe (Eds.), *Applied aviation psychology: Achievement, change and challenge* (pp. 209-218). Aldershot, UK: Ashgate.

Wiggins, M., & O'Hare, D. (1993). A skill-based approach to aeronautical decision-making. In R.A. Telfer (Ed.), *Aviation Instruction and Training* (pp. 430-475). Aldershot, UK: Gower.

Wiggins, M.W. & O'Hare, D. (1995). Expertise in aeronautical weather-related decision-making: A cross-sectional analysis of general aviation pilots. *Journal of Experimental Psychology: Applied, 1,* 305-320.

Woods, D.D. (1988). Coping with complexity: The psychology of human behaviour in complex systems. In L.P. Goodstein, H.B. Andersen, & S.E. Olsen (Eds.), *Tasks, errors and mental models* (pp. 128-148). London, UK: Taylor & Francis.

Woods, P. (1985). New songs played skilfully: Creativity and techniques in writing up qualitative research. In R.G. Burgess (Ed.), *Issues in educational research: Qualitative methods* (pp. 86-106). London, UK: The Flamer Press.

Index

For Product Safety Concerns and Information please contact our
EU representative GPSR@taylorandfrancis.com or Taylor & Francis
Verlag GmbH, Kaufingerstraße 24, 80331 München, Germany